A LIFE OF RHYME

A LIFE OF RHYME

David Harkins

ATHENA PRESS
LONDON

A LIFE OF RHYME
Copyright © David Harkins 2006

ISBN 1 84401 800 8

First Published 2006 by
ATHENA PRESS
Queen's House, 2 Holly Road
Twickenham TW1 4EG
United Kingdom

Printed for Athena Press

To my mother, Mary Harkins,
who was my greatest inspiration and is sadly missed.

Acknowledgements

I would like to thank Paul and Joseph Harkins for their help with this project. Thanks, guys!

To all my family, who are very important in my life; and all my friends.

Thank you to Douglas Davidson for his musical collaboration on 'Your Heart was with Somebody Else'.

And, finally... welcome to the world, Olivia May Roscoe!

The author, David Harkins

About the Author

I was born in Glasgow on 26 May 1962. I am the second oldest of ten children. My mother brought us up on her own as my father was never about for his family and played no part in our upbringing. It was tough for my mother bringing us up on a housing estate in Possilpark north Glasgow but she did it and she was the most fantastic person.

I attended St Cuthbert's Primary School in Possilpark and then St Augustine's Secondary School in Milton. After leaving school in 1978 I started working for the DIY chain Dodge City, later to become B&Q, in one of their many Glasgow stores. In 1985 I moved to Manchester in England and spent the next nine years working there, eventually qualifying to become a driving instructor.

I started writing poems about my life and family in Glasgow. This led me to start writing about most situations happening in my life and around me. My mother was my biggest influence and the inspiration for my writing.

I moved back to Glasgow in 1994. I had to give up work in 1999 due to an accident which severely damaged my back. I have since had two major operations to fix some of the damage. Unfortunately I live with chronic back pain but I'm learning to cope with it and writing for me is good therapy because it takes my mind off my back. I have a deep affection for Glasgow; I also love the history of Scotland and it's been a great form of inspiration for many of the poems I've written. I love reading historical novels and particularly books by Nigel Tranter and John Prebble.

I am currently working on a new volume of poetry which should be completed before the end of 2007.

David Harkins

Contents

A Brand New Year

Well, here we go for another year;
Twelve months have gone by.
Celebrating this brand new year
With a touch of scotch and rye.

When the time hits twelve o'clock
And the bells, they start to chime,
All you hear around the world
Is the sound of 'Auld Lang Syne'.

I hope this year brings better luck
Than the one that's just gone past,
And if happiness were to come my way
I hope that it would last.

The resolution I will make
Is as simple as it's clear:
To continue as a human being
Throughout this brand new year.

A Day in the Life

Living in a bedsit
Till I get my house.
Nearly jumping out my skin
When I see a mouse.

When I saw the landlord
We had a little chat.
That's when I decided
I had to get a cat.

Walking through a leisure park,
Everyone walking dogs.
Sitting at a nearby pond
Listening to the frogs.

Went to buy a lemon drink;
This will be my third.
Something's just dropped in it
From a cheeky little bird.

Off to catch a bus now
But I don't have the fare,
So I'll have to run home –
I wish I was a hare.

Someone playing music;
They probably think it's funky.
But I've heard better noises
From a little monkey.

Thought I'd seen a grizzly bear;
It was just a phoney.
Going to the pub now,
It's called the Horse and Pony.

A Friend

When you're ever feeling low
And you need someone to talk to,
Pick up the phone and call me
And I will comfort you.

As you know, I am your best friend,
Someone you can trust.
Having someone to talk to
Really is a must.

As a friend I don't make judgements;
I'm just here to help you out.
I'll always be here for you;
You only have to shout.

If you find your problems building up,
Get them off your chest.
As your friend, I'll listen;
I do not speak in jest.

Just call me if you need me;
On me you can depend.
And there's one last thing I want to say:
I'll always be your friend.

A Genuine Friend

Many years ago, I went on a David Urquart tour;
I met a really genuine couple, that's for sure.
On that trip we had some brilliant weather,
And with Peter and Aggie, I had a wee blether.

I didn't know then, I really must say,
That I'd still be in touch to this very day.
They have a great wee friend, a man called Bobby,
And going down to the woody is big Peter's hobby.

Usually, once a month, I go for my tea;
Aggie really knows how to spoil me.
I really can't resist the meals that she makes,
And the highlight for me is definitely her steak.

I'll never forget one day, because
Over my steak I poured raspberry sauce.

Colin's a very nice guy – that's their son –
They both are so proud he's given them a grandson.
I can see why they are really glad;
He really is a bonnie wee lad.

If Peter was ever given three wishes,
I know one would be to avoid the dishes.
Aggie says I'm a really nice bloke,
But she tells me to keep quiet if I tell her a joke.

I've seen her emotional, and have a wee greet;
She's the most caring person you ever will meet.
With Peter and Aggie, you get what you see,
And it's that special quality that's important to me.

From the bottom of my heart, my love I will send;
Thank you, Peter and Aggie, from your genuine friend.

A Genuine Scot

This country of mine I love so well;
My feelings for Scotland I just have to tell.
Its hills and its glens are a sight to be seen,
From John O'Groats to Gretna Green.

Scots are real friendly people, who'll give you no hassle,
And there's nothing to beat a real Scottish castle!
Historical monuments all over this land;
Just speak to our tourist board – they'll give you a hand.

For places to go, you'll find there are lots;
You'll enjoy yourself in the land of the Scots.
Up in the Orkneys, or the Western Isles,
There's so much to see, if you travel the miles.

Edinburgh's the capital, but Glasgow's the place,
For the friendliest people you ever will face.
In this land of the thistle and heather,
It's just a pity we don't always have the weather.

Many of the tourists to Loch Lomond are Yanks;
They just can't resist our beautiful bonnie banks.
If there are friendlier people than here in this land,
There's no doubt in my mind you'll find them in Ireland.

But for my country and the love I have got,
I'm proud to call myself a genuine Scot.

A Glasgow Thing

A place where ships were a common sight,
A place where gangs would meet to fight,
A place where drunks felt right at home
A place where poverty seems to roam:
It's just a Glasgow thing.

A place with tenements and high-rise flats,
A place not used to aristocrats,
A place where buildings are very old,
A place where winter is really cold:
It's just a Glasgow thing.

A place that's spoke of in song and verse,
A place where the people are the salt of the earth,
A place where the accent is strong and fast,
A place where memories will always last:
It's just a Glasgow thing.

A place I miss when I go away,
A place where I will return someday,
A place that really must be seen,
A place where religion is blue or green:
It's just a Glasgow thing.

A Life of Hell

I'm starting to feel the pressure
Being off work brings:
All the signs of depression
And many other things.

I can't be bothered with anything;
I really feel like crap.
It seems I've really changed
From being a cheerful chap.

I try to keep my head up,
Telling myself things will improve,
But it isn't always easy
When you just aren't in the groove.

I get annoyed with little things,
I just don't have control.
It's like four walls are closing in;
I'm trapped inside a hole.

At this present moment in time,
I feel I have to tell,
The only life I am living
Is a life of hell.

A Lifetime

Between the ages of one and nine
You're just finding your way,
And between the ages of ten and nineteen
Puberty has a say.

Between the ages of twenty and twenty-nine
With your pals you hit the town,
And between the ages of thirty and thirty-nine
You're hoping to be settled down.

Between the ages of forty and forty-nine
You should definitely be mature,
And between the ages of fifty and fifty-nine
You'll have a middle-age spread for sure.

Between the ages of sixty and sixty-nine
You'll have white hair on your head,
And between the ages of seventy and seventy-nine
You're fortunate not to be dead.

Between the ages of eighty and eighty-nine
It's definitely time to chuck it,
And between the ages of ninety and one hundred
It's time you kicked the bucket.

A Little Bit of Kindness

A little bit of kindness
Goes a long, long way.
A little bit of kindness
Makes you feel good each day.

A little bit of kindness
Is not too much to ask.
A little bit of kindness
Is such a simple task.

A little bit of kindness
Makes others feel much better.
A little bit of kindness
Can be spread in a letter.

A little bit of kindness
Is not too much to give.
A little bit of kindness
Is the way we all should live.

A little bit of kindness
Is something we all have.
A little bit of kindness
Will always make us laugh.

A little bit of kindness
Is sometimes hard to find;
Surely it's not much to ask
To be a little kind?

A Man called Shane

I write this poem about a man called Shane;
He's really talented, though some would say insane.
He's written the most beautiful songs you'll ever hear,
But he's destroying himself, and this I fear.

He formed a group, they were called the Pogues;
But many people just saw them as rogues.
Onstage, they were seen as Irish punks,
And written off as nothing but drunks.

But Shane's the kind of guy who doesn't give a toss;
He just tells them all to go and piss off.
His songs are stories of Irish life,
Of all the hardships, troubles and strife.

His lifestyle is destructive and that is sad,
But no one could write a more beautiful ballad.
He's most influential when he's out of his head
But I dread the day when I'm told he is dead.

I'm not trying to worship him or kiss his arse,
But I can't help admiring the talent he has.
I don't care if people think he's a clown;
I just love the music of Shane MacGowan.

To finish this poem I'll make it quite plain:
It's just my wee tribute to a man called Shane.

A Pain in the Back

I'm lying here in agony, suffering this pain;
My back is driving me completely insane.
Although it's not enough to make me want to die,
It's enough to bring me to my knees and make me want to
    cry.

Instead of being up and feeling full of zest,
It's getting me down and making me depressed.
I've tried all kinds of treatment, nothing does the trick;
Nothing seems to help me once my back goes click.

Doctors say, 'Just rest', but they haven't got a clue.
And if doctors cannot help me, what else can I do?
I don't want to leave my job and I don't want the sack,
But I might have to give it up because of my bad back.

Maybe there is hope; my sister has a plan,
To go to see a specialist by the name of Dr Chan.
His methods are alternative, but what have I got to lose?
Being in my position, I can't afford to choose.

After a couple of sessions down at his Ayrshire practice,
I can honestly say I'm feeling a little bit more active.
Although it's early days, I have a little hope
That as far as my back is concerned, I'll soon be able to
    cope.

Thanks to all the family, for everything you've done;
I thank you all for being there, each and every one.
In giving me hope, you all have played your part;
So thank you very much, from the bottom of my heart.

A Proposal in Paris

A romantic setting by the Eiffel tower,
Where I gave you a lovely summer flower.
In this city of romance and wine,
I asked the question: would you be mine?

You said you would love to be my wife,
Because with me you wanted to spend your life.
All around the birds did sing
As on your finger I placed a ring.

To you my love, I just want to say:
I never will forget this day.
It's here in Paris I wanted to propose.
I felt it was right, because we are so close.

Apart, I hope we're never,
I want to be with you for ever.
As long as I live there's one thing I'll bet:
This day in Paris I'll never forget.

When we go back home our families will guess
That I asked for your hand, and you said yes.
I love you so much, I know that it's right
To make a commitment to you this night.

In this land of madames and monsieurs,
Is where I decided to be for ever yours.
There's one more thing I have to do:
As I look into your eyes, I'll just say, 'Thank you.'

A Strange Relation

It's strange that we're related
For I know not who you are.
You've always been so distant;
Why are you so far?

There must have been a reason
To stay away from me;
You had to make a choice.
That choice was to flee.

You never kept in contact;
Somehow I didn't mind,
Because from what I can remember
You were never very kind.

It seems you had another life
That didn't include your kin;
One that had you making decisions
From many bottles of gin.

I guess you must have made a mistake,
Dumping us for the boozer,
For now I hear you're on your own
And living like a loser.

You mustn't think I hate you –
That's not the way I am –
But if you wonder what I think of you
I couldn't give a damn.

I'm not trying to condemn you
By making this declaration,
But if someone asks me who you are,
I reply, 'A strange relation.'

A Summer's Day

This morning I had a look outside;
The sky was clear and blue.
The sun was shining brightly
As I admired the scenic view.

All the flowers were blooming,
The grass was fresh and green.
The birds were singing loudly;
There were many to be seen.

This beautiful summer morning
Life seems so worthwhile;
This wonderful summer weather
Makes me want to smile.

It's such a change from winter
When things are dull and grey;
There's nothing better in this life
Than a lovely summer's day.

A Total Stranger

This is the story of my father, as seen through my eyes.
I'd say there were good times, but I'd be telling lies.
He had no time for his family, which was very sad.
I might be his son, but he was never my dad.

He was never about to protect us from danger;
He was nothing to me but a total stranger.
He lived for his pals, so his family were shunned;
He treated us like shit, and that left us stunned.

He thought he was God's gift, gallivanting here and there;
But when it came to his family, he had nothing to share.
When I was seriously ill in a hospital bed,
For all he cared, I could have been dead.

Mum brought us up; he played no part.
All he ever did was break her heart.
She really didn't deserve a rat like him;
The way he treated her was a bloody sin.

He's sorry now, but it's all too late;
He's a sad old man in a sorry state.
It could have been different if he'd kept in touch,
But he never even bothered to do that much.

I feel sorry for him now because he's in a bit of a state,
Although I should be feeling nothing but hate.
But I'll never forget the past, and the damage he's done;
He's just a total stranger, and that's from his son.

A Town called Ullapool

A little town called Ullapool
Where I once spent a day,
Surrounded by beautiful scenery,
Just took my breath away.

It's up in the north-west of Scotland
And the buildings are mostly white.
The town is clean and tidy
And the locals are polite.

It attracts many tourists
During the summer season,
But it's great to go there any time;
You do not need a reason.

So if you need a holiday,
Or the kids have time off school,
Do yourself a favour
And visit a town called Ullapool.

A Wee Wino

What a day! Time for a bit of relaxing;
Today has been stressful, tiresome and taxing.
I need a drink, well, a wee glass of wine;
It helps me relax time after time.

It's just a wee tonic I take now and then,
It helps me unwind, now and again.
I hope you don't think that I'm a wee wino,
Just because I end up asleep on the lino.

I wake up with a hangover, but it's no big deal;
I'll have a wee glass later, along with my meal.
I know what I'm doing, I'm well in control,
As long as I remember to sign on the dole.

Passing the boozer's no problem to me;
I don't need to go in there for a drink, you see.
I'm not an alcoholic and that is final,
But I guess I'll admit to being a wee wino.

Above the Clouds

Flying high above the clouds,
Far away from all the crowds.
Destination: USA
And the beautiful San Francisco Bay.

Many hours up in the sky,
Above the clouds, flying high.
Looking at the clouds below,
They look so much like fluffy snow.

Above the clouds, out of sight
Flying all through the night.
Amazing thing, this aeroplane
But I would feel safer on a train.

There's not much point being frantic –
We're almost halfway across the Atlantic.
People travel in the ships below
But the ships are travelling very slow.

Flying there might take a day
But it really is the fastest way.
Pilot announces he is descending
Below the clouds; the journey's ending.

Alba

Look at the beauty our eyes can see!
This feeling of being completely free;
The Alba mountains I'd love to climb
And used to do from time to time.

So many lochs – I love them all –
And the sight of a wondrous waterfall.
The highland heather and so much more;
The Alba sayings I've heard afore.

The different tartans that divide the clans,
The Alba music and highland dance.
The rugged look of real hard graft
Seen on faces not so daft.

The warm embrace from far and wide
From Scots who are so full of pride.
Marvellous beauty from the highlands to the lower
The English are lucky to live next door.

We welcome them with open arms,
As they do us with all their charms.
An ancient land we've always been;
Alba's a place that must be seen.

All Kinds of People

It takes all kinds of people
To make things as they are;
The ones who have got nothing
And the ones who have got far.

People are so different;
No two are the same.
Then again, if we were
That would be a shame.

Because different personalities
Is something we must have.
Some people will make you cry;
Some will make you laugh.

Some people are always happy;
Some are always sad.
I'm sure it has something to do
With the life that they have had.

Some people keep on growing
Until they're very tall,
But they still don't outnumber
The ones who are small.

Many different styles of hair;
Many different colours,
And those who are bald
Make up the others.

Black or white, yellow or brown,
Everyone has a say.
It takes all kinds of people
To make the world that way.

Alone

My world is falling in on me
Before my very eyes.
I'm shouting out for help
But no one hears my cries.

Why can no one hear me?
I do not understand.
I do not ask for money,
Just a helping hand.

A little bit of someone's time,
This is all I ask.
But no one has come near me
To help me with my task.

Maybe I have myself to blame,
For friends, I don't have many.
In fact, to be quite honest,
I really don't have any.

Now that I am older
And time is passing by,
I wish that there was someone's hand
To hold before I die.

An Innocent Man

Accused of a crime I didn't commit
And sentenced to a life inside;
I'll never survive in this small cell,
Which is twelve by ten feet wide.

My life is not worth living
As long as I'm in jail.
While my lawyer appeals on my behalf,
I hope to get out on bail.

This is such a miscarriage of justice;
I'm innocent, for goodness' sake!
To be inside for nothing
Is just too hard to take.

I demand to have a re-trial
So justice can be done!
I really need to prove to you
That I'm not the guilty one.

Lots of evidence was kept from court
That would prove it wasn't me.
If it was available for the jury
I know I would be free.

I swear to you I'm innocent;
Another has done this crime.
But instead of catching the guilty one
It's me who's doing time.

I've lost my faith in justice
But I'll be doing what I can
To prove to those who doubt me
That I am an innocent man.

An Irishman's Farewell to Glasgow

Now I am leaving Glasgow,
Though it's hard for me to do,
For I have to go to Ireland
And now I'm feeling blue.

I've seen so many changes
To the dear green place I love,
But I'm going back to Ireland
For now my times are tough.

I came here forty years ago
And I've always felt at home.
But since my wife passed away
I've been left here on my own.

I still have my family in Ireland
And it's there I have to be.
For now I'm old and lonely
And, also, I cannot see.

I recently lost my eyesight,
And now I'm totally blind,
So going back to my family
Is for my own peace of mind.

There's one more thing I want to say
That I want you all to know:
Until the day I die
I will love the people of Glasgow.

Angel

I've never heard the voice of an angel
But I still know they are there;
I've never seen one with my eyes
But I don't really care.

I know within my heart of hearts
That angels do exist,
Because many times, throughout my life,
By an angel I have been kissed.

I've stared at death so many times
And yet I am still here;
It's all thanks to an angel
That I've overcome my fear.

They do their job in silence,
Without you even knowing.
I guess the fact that I'm alive
Means it's not my time for going.

So, for my guardian angel
I have just one thing to say:
Thanks for looking after me
And keeping me safe this day.

Assembly

All lined up on hearing the bell;
Headmaster asks, 'Is everyone well?'
'Yes sir!' was the gleeful reply,
Though I was worried about my tie.

Although I'd been shown how to do a knot,
When I put it on, I'd totally forgot.
'Fix your tie,' the headmaster said.
Everyone looked; my face went red.

He saw me struggling, then said, 'Come here.'
I approached him with a little fear.
He fixed my tie, I felt so daft;
Going back to my seat, everyone laughed.

Maybe I felt daft because I'm a sensitive creature,
Or maybe it's because I am the teacher.

At Peace

Every time I think of you
A tear comes to my eye.
I know you're in a better place
So I've stopped asking, 'Why?'

No more do you suffer
This thing that we call pain.
What we were to lose
Heaven was to gain.

I know you're at peace now
Since the Lord's call.
I just wanted to say
I love you, that's all.

At the Top

A whole new world lies ahead;
I'll leave the old behind.
I'm going to make a new start;
I've new challenges to find.

I'm really feeling positive.
My life is going great –
So different to how it used to be,
Though it's partly down to fate.

But fate is just a small part;
I have to make it work.
But if I fail to make it
Does that mean I'm a berk?

But I'm not thinking of failure;
I'm determined to succeed.
I really feel it deep within
And success I hope to breed.

So if I focus on success
And my hunger doesn't stop,
I don't think it will be too long
Till I am at the top.

Baby

Little baby cries, looking for a feed;
Mummy heats a bottle, putting down her read.
Baby now is silent, as she has her feed.
Nappy now needs changing; just another need.

Baby now is smiling, happy with her lot;
Mummy is also happy with the bundle of joy she's got.
Daddy plays with baby, saying, 'Coochie coo.'
Baby looks at Daddy; thinks he's had a few.

Baby's getting tired, time for beddy-byes;
Mummy puts her into bed; baby closes eyes.
Daddy looks at Mummy, winking with his eye,
Heading for the bedroom, when baby starts to cry.

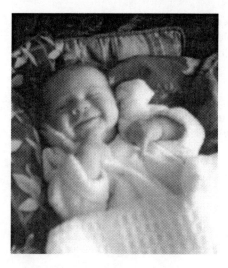

Back to Normal

As I face this operation
So much goes through my mind:
Will it be a complete success?
Will the pain be left behind?

I'm actually quite excited,
I really cannot wait.
I'm sure there'll be so much I can do
That I haven't done of late.

I've suffered this for fifteen years;
Each year it gets much worse.
Since falling off 'that' ladder
My back has been a curse.

But now I know the problem
And it needs the surgeon's knife,
But I know that when he's finished
I'll have a better life.

It's strange that one small accident
Has caused me so much grief;
For years I've had to suffer
But now I have belief.

The problem will be sorted;
I'm pretty sure of that.
And for the man responsible
I do take off my hat.

You've given me the hope
For so long I've desired,
I'll no longer need the drugs
That always make me tired.

I promise to make the most of it
When my back is strong enough.
I'll feel I've got my life again
And do all the things I love.

Bad to Good

I found it in my heart today
To make a little sacrifice,
Though some say this decision
Might not be very wise.

I do not care what people think;
This is just my choice.
But no one has come forward
To let me hear their voice.

Maybe they speak in whispers
Or talk behind my back.
The only thing that I would say:
Guts are what they lack.

Everyone has the right
To live the life they want.
I have made my decision
And confirmed it at the font.

My life is so much better
Since I made this change.
The satisfaction that I get
Covers a wider range.

I gave my heart to Jesus
That is what I've done.
I've turned away from evil,
The devil now I shun.

If people want to make a change
Others should not be rude.
Instead they would be better
Changing from bad to good.

Beautiful British Columbia

I've been to Canada, a place called BC;
It's a beautiful province you really must see.
There's Vancouver Island, a sight to behold,
And, in wintertime, it isn't too cold.

Vancouver itself is a beautiful sight,
Especially when it's lit up at night.
You can go in your car or your station wagon,
And visit the tranquillity of the Okanogan.

If you carry on eastwards to the Kootenay,
You can spend time there and have a wonderful day.
The British Columbia Rockies: a magnificent scene;
You'll want to go back, once you have been.

If you go to the high country, there's more than a chance
That most of the people will own a big ranch.
There's still more to see; you thought I'd forgotten?
But how could I forget the Caribou-Chilcotin.

Moving further on, you've got to see the rest,
And head into the land of North by North-west.
Finally, if you decide to see British Columbia my way,
Head for Peace River and Alaska Highway.

Well, that is the province of Canada, you see,
The one that they call beautiful BC.

Belfast

Walking through Belfast
I didn't feel at ease;
Soldiers there with weapons
Trying to keep the peace.

But people just resent them,
And say they have no right
To be on the streets of Belfast
Every day and night.

They are only doing their job;
They're not there out of choice.
I'm sure they'd rather be somewhere else
But they haven't got a voice.

I think the British government
Should now withdraw their forces;
The Irish can police themselves
With their own resources.

With the army out of Ireland
I'm sure that peace can last.
Then maybe I will feel at ease
Walking through Belfast.

Betrayed

I remember the day you came into my life;
The sun was splitting the skies.
We had many years of happiness
And then came the lies.

I thought we'd always be as one,
I thought you felt the same.
How blind I was not to see
Your foolish little game!

Although you've really let me down
I don't feel any hate;
I'm just sad you didn't tell me
Before it was too late.

If someone else comes into my life
The one thing that's a must:
That right from the very beginning
There's honesty and trust.

But I doubt if I could fall in love
The way I did before.
I gave to you my everything
Now my heart is for ever sore.

Book of Rhyme

A man walks towards me
Holding out his hand.
He asks me where I'm going;
I tell him, 'Another land.'

He says, 'Do not be hasty,
This is not your time.
You have so much to offer
With your book of rhyme.'

'But no one wants to read it,'
Was my quick reply.
He said it would be published
Then looked up to the sky.

'Do not take him, Father!
He has so much to give,
With his talent for writing
It's right to let him live.'

Suddenly, the man disappears,
He's completely out of sight.
Then I wake up from a dream
And suddenly I want to write.

I'll have to heed the warning
And do more with my time.
I'll continue to keep on writing
And complete my book of rhyme.

Broken Trust

Walk away and don't come back
I do not want you here.
You cause me so much anger
And this is what I fear.

You used to be so gentle
But suddenly you have changed,
Almost to the point
Where I think you are deranged.

I do not need the hassle
You always seem to cause.
I'll just be glad to see you go,
I will not feel the loss.

The love I had is gone now;
You've ruined what we had.
You took me to the very edge,
All you are is bad.

Don't think I will change my mind;
I've taken far too much.
I only hope the likes of you
I never again will touch.

I wouldn't even weep for you
If I heard that you were dust.
This is all I think of you
Since the day you broke my trust.

Callum

Little Callum Taylor,
A bonnie little lad,
Brings joy to his mum, Lorna
And Colin, who's his dad.

He is a little character
Who has a lot of style,
And you just can't help admiring
His lovely little smile.

I know God will protect him
And keep him well and safe,
This future little Ranger
Who's really very brave.

So, Callum, keep on smiling
Like only you can do.
I wrote this little poem
Especially for you.

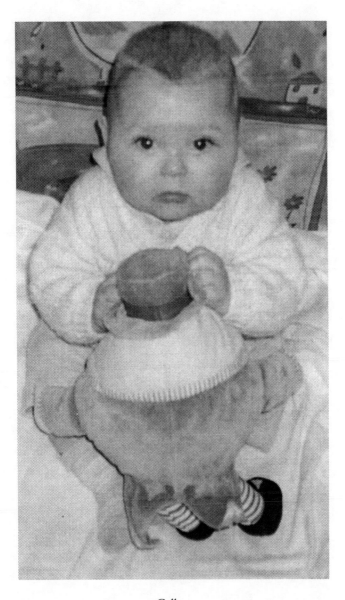

Callum

Caps

I collect all sorts of skip hats
From everywhere I've been.
It's just a way of life to me;
They are all there to be seen.

From America and Canada
Belgium, France and Spain,
Of all the caps that I collect
There aren't two the same.

I've been given caps at home
And had some sent from Oz.
The more I get from my friends
Only helps my cause.

There are millions of caps in this world,
I wish I had them all,
But I know that isn't possible;
There's not enough room on my wall.

Reebok caps, Nike caps;
Some say they're the best.
But in with my collection
They're equal with the rest.

I've got about three hundred,
But will not stop at that;
In another day or two
I'll have another skip hat.

People might say I'm crazy
I would agree, perhaps,
But I couldn't give a monkey's:
I'll keep collecting caps.

Cartoons

The first time I ever saw a cartoon on the telly,
It was a cat and mouse called *Tom and Jerry*,
Causing havoc and being funny.
There was also a rabbit called Bugs Bunny.

From out of nothing, characters were born.
One of the best was Foghorn Leghorn.
There was spinach-eating Popeye the Sailor Man,
And that little rascal, Yosemite Sam.

Dastardly and Mutley are well-known faces,
Who started out in the *Whacky Races*.
Sylvester the Cat and Tweety Pie;
Beep! Beep! Wile E Coyote would try and try.

So many cartoons, I've named a few,
But there's also *The Flintstones* and *Scooby Doo*.
Cartoons are fun and full of jokes,
So keep on enjoying them. That's all folks!

Change

Looking at the life I have
I cannot help but laugh.
It isn't funny, but, nonetheless,
Everyone gets into a little mess.

But things will change, just wait and see,
For I am strong – I have to be.
A brand new path I wish to take;
I'll make it happen for goodness' sake.

No more drinks of alcohol;
All it does is make me fall.
No more lies; I've told enough.
No more times of living rough.

All bad memories will have to go.
It will take time, of course, I know.
But change will come, I know it will;
I've had enough of standing still.

It might not happen overnight
But I will make sure I do it right.
I can't imagine staying this way
So instead of tomorrow I'll start today.

There may be friends I'll leave behind,
But new friends I will surely find.
I know at first it may be strange
But I'll feel better for the change.

Childhood Days, Happy Days

Childhood days are happy days,
The best days you can have.
It's great to see the children happy,
It's great to hear them laugh.

Childhood days are precious;
Enjoy them while you can,
Because one day you will grow up
To be a woman or a man.

No matter where you go to,
All the different places,
It's always great to see
Those happy smiling faces.

I hope that all the children
Enjoy their childhood phase,
Because nothing can compare
To all those happy days.

Christmas Time

Christmas time is here again;
It comes around so fast.
It doesn't seem like twelve months
Since I celebrated the last.

Although a time for children,
Adults love it too.
But they prefer the New Year
When they can have a few.

A time for getting presents,
For children to enjoy.
It's great to see their faces
When they unwrap a brand new toy.

Lots of films on telly;
Laughter all around.
Lots of festive music;
Quite a lovely sound.

Many people struggle,
But still they give so much.
They have to be admired
For having a special touch.

So as the festive spirit
Really begins to grow,
Don't forget Jesus Christ –
It's because of him, you know.

Colours

Imagine a world without colours
Where everything was black and white,
Somehow it's hard to imagine;
It just wouldn't seem right.

We need to see a blue sky
On a bright and sunny day,
Unless, of course, it's raining
Then usually the sky is grey.

So many colourful flowers,
They really must be seen;
And all the different trees
Where all the leaves are green.

So many beautiful colours,
Including yellow, orange and red;
We all take them for granted,
It really must be said.

But imagine if you couldn't see;
Imagine if you were blind,
To never see all those colours
Well, that would be very unkind.

Crimebusters

They gave us Simon Templar;
They gave us Jason King.
If you want a murder solved
Just give them a ring.

Remembering *The Champions*
Richard, Craig and Sharron,
They had people on the run
And don't forget the Baron.

Remember *The Persuaders*?
Always in a chase.
McGill's car wasn't up to much
He was a man in a suitcase.

Sometimes the Man from UNCLE
Was taken for a ride,
But this was quickly sorted out
By a man called Ironside.

No mission was impossible,
They all had their own styles.
Now they give us *Hart to Hart*
And *The Rockford Files*.

Bring back the heroes of yesteryear,
And not this mumbo-jumbo.
At least we've still got someone good
And that's Lieutenant Columbo.

I hear that there's a bank been robbed;
Will they catch the robbers?
No one special on the job,
Just the normal coppers.

Crooners

Sinatra was the guv'nor,
The master of all he surveyed.
The Chairman packed them out
Wherever he had played.

Dean was also a master,
One of the all-time greats;
Along with Frank and Sammy
They were a good bunch of mates.

Then there's Andy Williams
A home lovin' man' with class;
And Mr Tom Jones
With his 'green, green grass'.

Engelbert Humperdinck –
Of him I'm sure you'll know –
And, of course, another genius,
A man called Matt Monro.

Also, Julio Iglesias,
With all the girls he's loved before,
And not to forget the Frenchman:
Monsieur Charles Aznavour.

Remember Al Martino,
With his 'Spanish eyes'?
And Mr Tony Bennett,
The 'stranger in Paradise'.

They sang their songs with passion,
Singing from the soul.
Especially one in particular
The unforgettable' Nat King Cole.

Masters Crosby and Como
(Did you think that I'd forget?)
Make up all the crooners
Who really had the lot.

Cul-de-sac

I don't know where I'm going
While driving down this road.
I do not have my brain switched on;
It's in an empty mode.

I did not see the traffic sign,
Which warns what lies ahead.
I haven't been this way before
So I'll ask someone instead.

I can't go left, I can't go right
I can't just stop and reverse;
If someone was behind me,
I might cause them to swerve.

I stop to ask a pedestrian
Who says I must turn back.
It's only now I realise what he means;
I am in a cul-de-sac.

Death of the Innocents

A madman with a gun,
Who we now know was insane,
Shot dead sixteen children
In the silence of Dunblane.

He walked into their school
Without a single care.
He fired at the children
And death was everywhere.

Whatever did possess him
To commit this evil crime;
To kill these innocent children
And take away their time?

The madman took his own life;
A very cowardly act.
He'd have been murdered 'inside' anyway:
That is just a fact.

He also killed their teacher,
Who tried her best to protect.
He didn't stop to think
The lives he would affect.

Those sixteen little angels
Are all with God above;
They can't be hurt any more
They're in a place of love.

The children who survived
Will always have the nightmare.
What they saw that fateful day
Just seems so unfair.

For everyone involved,
It really was a shame.
I hope we never see again
A massacre like Dunblane.

Del Boy

This is the story of Del Boy,
The independent trader.
If you're looking for a bargain
He's the man to cater.

It isn't always kosher
The things that he will sell,
But that really doesn't bother
This dodgy dealer, Del.

Del Boy is a great guy,
Definitely not a rotter.
Along with the plonker Rodney
They make up the Brothers Trotter.

There's also Uncle Albert
The able-bodied seaman,
Then Del's little Damien
Who Rodney thinks is a demon.

The boys go down the market
Where Del Boy makes his cash,
The first sign of a copper
And Del Boy makes a dash.

Their little Reliant Robin
Is how they get about;
It's certainly seen its day,
That's without a doubt.

Off they go to their local,
It's called the Nag's Head pub.
Del likes his cocktails
But doesn't like Mike's grub.

Del's a little chancer
With a heart of gold,
Although he never pays the tax
On anything he's sold.

When it comes to making money,
Del is always there,
And swears that by this time next year
He'll be a millionaire.

This lovable rogue from Peckham
Is determined to make it bigger,
But he'll never forget his friends
Especially one called Trigger.

All his little sayings,
'Lovely jubbly', and '*Au contraire*',
Made *Only Fools and Horses*
What it is today.

I really love this comedy;
It brings me lots of joy,
The story of the Trotters
And most of all Del Boy.

Depressed

So much scares me in this life
But I don't let anyone know;
I use my humour to cover it up
But that is just a show.

If people could see how I really am,
They'd see I'm very weak,
Because deep down I really know
My future's very bleak.

I cannot help but worry;
It's just the way I am.
But I'm not in a state of panic
I'm actually very calm.

I just take one day at a time
And, whatever comes my way,
I try to deal with it the best I can
And hope to get through the day.

I can't really plan ahead;
That would be tempting fate.
The pressure that would put on me
Would just be far too great.

Some can cope better than others
And take things in their stride;
To lean on someone's shoulder
Would only hurt my pride.

Someday I'll talk to someone
And get it off my chest,
But until I'm able to do that
I'll continue to feel depressed.

Diary

Early Monday morning
Starts another day.
Have a little breakfast
To help me on my way.

Tuesday it was raining;
I hate it when it pours.
I guess I'll have to stay in
And do some household chores.

Wednesday the weather's better;
I'll go out for a walk,
Either to the park
Or just around the block.

Today I see the doctor;
It's Thursday afternoon.
I'm waiting for an operation;
I hope to have it soon.

Friday's here already;
A week has just gone past.
I really don't believe it,
The time goes by so fast.

Saturday starts the weekend;
Time to get some shopping.
I'll buy a frozen pizza
With a pepperoni topping.

Sunday ends the weekend;
Seven days gone by.
I'll put it in my diary
But I really don't know why.

Disasters

They say we live in a safer world;
I'm not sure if it's true.
Looking back at recent disasters
There's been a lot more than a few.

I was shocked about the ferry
And what was to follow
Was just as scary.

Piper Alpha, what a scare;
Thank God my brother wasn't there.

The Clapham train crash
The King's Cross fire;
The amount of deaths was getting higher.

Remember Lockerbie, and Flight 103?
A tragic sight for all to see.

The M1 plane crash,
More lives were taken;
Then the earthquakes –
The world was shaken.

Thinking back, oh what a shame,
And then we had that football game.
To all the families, my love I send;
Will the disasters ever end?

All these sights of frightful terror,
And mostly because of human error.

Down and Out

Out on the street with nowhere to go;
I don't think life gets any more low.
Begging for money for drink and fags,
With nothing to wear except these rags.

Cardboard boxes to shelter from the cold,
Eating food from bins covered in mould.
How the hell did I get into this state?
Were the pressures of life just too great?

Is it just my destiny and meant to be?
I've got perfect eyesight yet I cannot see.
My life is worthless and I'm to blame,
And I know I should hang my head in shame.

The way I am is self-inflicted,
When to alcohol I got addicted.
It's ruined my life without a doubt;
Now all I am is a down and out.

Dream

Dreaming in my bed at night,
Dreaming as I dream;
Is it wrong to dream like this?
Is it wrong to dream?

No one knows why we dream,
No one knows at all.
When I have a brilliant dream
I give my mum a call.

In this world I live in
There's not a lot I've seen;
If I sleep for long enough
I'll see it in my dream.

As I'm getting older,
This is how it seems.
Dreaming usually happens
When you're in your teens.

I'm dreaming only good dreams
But I don't really care;
I'll only start to worry
If this is just… a nightmare.

Driving in the Countryside

Driving in the countryside,
Everything is thriving.
A little bit of music
While I do my driving.

Drive out of the busy towns,
Drive to somewhere quiet.
The best place is the countryside;
You really ought to try it.

Everything in order,
Passenger by my side,
Loving every minute
Of the countryside.

Getting pretty late now,
Quite a lot I've seen.
On my way back home;
Oh, what a day it's been!

If you want to be alone,
If you want to hide,
You'll feel terrific driving
In the countryside.

Droopy drawers

Droopy Drawers

I call you Little Droopy Drawers;
You look at me with a frown.
But the reason that I call you that
Is because your pants keep falling down.

Maybe they're too big for you,
Or your bottom needs some air;
They don't just fall down in the house,
They fall down everywhere.

Whatever people may think,
I love you just the same.
But I hope that when you're older
Droopy Drawers isn't your name.

Drugs

There are too many people
Dying because of drugs.
Many take them because they're ill;
Many because they're mugs.

Many people take them
Because they cannot cope.
Others say there's nothing wrong
With just a little dope.

People who use cannabis
Say I'm only being rash.
They say there's nothing wrong
With just a little hash.

I've seen some desperate addicts
Trying to find a vein
To inject a fix of heroin,
Or snorting some cocaine.

Many lives are wasted,
Most of them are young.
Drug dealers everywhere
Really should be hung.

They are making lots of money
From this evil trade,
Living a life of luxury
From all the cash they've made.

They cannot have a conscience
To ask the question: 'Why?'
While their profits are growing,
Someone else will die.

So don't be taken in
By these mindless thugs.
You'll only ruin your life
Getting into drugs.

Dumped

She made me feel important,
I loved her oh so much.
Then one day she turned from me,
She didn't want to touch.

This sudden act of coldness;
Was it something that I'd done?
I thought she really liked me;
We were having so much fun.

Maybe I gave her too much love
And she didn't have an answer,
Or maybe she just looked at me
And thought I was a chancer.

But still she let me love her
And made me feel a king.
But I didn't know by dumping me
The sadness she would bring.

I thought I'd make her happy
But this was not to be.
I hope that someone makes her happy;
I'm just sorry it's not me.

In my heart I'll always love her
But I know I must go on.
I just didn't think I'd feel like this,
But I do, now that she's gone.

When someone shuts you out their life
You feel like you've been thumped.
I'm not ashamed to say to you,
Yes! I have been dumped.

Enough

When I looked for you,
You were not there,
Why is it you
Just don't seem to care?

The way that you act
Is tearing us apart,
When all I did was love you
With all of my heart.

But you just carry on
Playing your game;
How would you feel
If I did the same?

I'm getting so tired
Of the way you behave;
When I am about,
You think I'm your slave.

I'm taking no more
Of all that stuff.
I'm getting out;
I've had enough.

I won't be coming back
For a life of hell.
Without you in my life
I'll do very well.

I hope you are happy,
We're no longer together,
And that's the way it will be
For ever and ever.

Every Dog has its Day

You have the nerve to say to me
That I'm just a waste of space;
But I can hold my head up,
Convinced I'm no disgrace.

I may not be outgoing
And I like to be on my own,
But I have a heart that's tender,
Not a heart of stone.

The things you say can hurt me;
You really can be cruel.
At times I think you must enjoy
Making me look a fool.

Do you mean to be malicious,
The way you put me down?
Why don't you complete the job,
And really go to town?

Push me when I'm falling,
Rub salt into my wound;
For all it really matters
I might as well be doomed.

If you knew how much you hurt me,
Would you continue on this way?
Just try to remember the saying:
Every dog has its day.

Everything

There was a time when I had something,
But these days I have nothing.
I'm not asking for everything,
But I'd gladly accept anything.

Although I would probably take anything,
I do not wish for everything.
I can still get by with nothing
But it helps if I have a little something.

I would probably give up anything
To have a little something;
But it doesn't have to be everything
Because I'll still be here with nothing.

So, if I can survive with nothing,
Then I don't need anything;
Not even a little something,
Because one day I'll have everything.

Everything Lost

I'm driving through the pouring rain
Late for where I'm going,
But what was to lie up ahead
I had no way of knowing.

The speed that I was driving at
To me was not too fast,
But how wrong I was,
For that journey would be my last.

Approaching a bend, I did not see
I'd lost complete control;
I collided with another car.
The crash then took its toll.

Paralysed for ever
Never again to walk;
And left with permanent brain damage,
I never again will talk.

A lifetime in this wheelchair
Is all that's left in store.
I didn't ask for this in life;
I wanted so much more.

The driver of the other car
Got a better deal.
I see him as the lucky one;
He died behind the wheel.

The accident wasn't his fault;
It was I who caused his death,
And I know I'll have to live with it
Till I draw my final breath.

I guess I do deserve this
For the heartache I have caused.
I once had so much in my life,
Now everything I've lost.

Face the Fear

No more looking back;
Time to move ahead.
I'm looking to the future;
What's in the past is dead.

My life before was empty,
Nothing filled my heart.
But now I see the way ahead
And now's the time to start.

I thought I'd never see the day
I'd leave the past behind.
The life I had before today
Wasn't very kind.

Due to problems with my health,
Plans I could not make.
But now my problems are sorted out,
Now a positive view I take.

So no more looking back for me;
My way ahead is clear.
It's great to have this feeling
That I have faced the fear.

Faithful Carpet

I hope you don't mind
If I give you a clean;
You are looking a bit dirty,
Know what I mean?

You've been like this
Since you were new;
People just seem
To walk all over you.

You've put up with so much
In your short life;
When I first saw you
You were cut with a knife.

You are there every day
When I come home;
With you in the house
I'm never alone.

Do not worry, dear friend,
As I try to manoeuvre
Over your surface
With this noisy Hoover.

Falling

It's true I'm forever falling
As each day passes by.
I no longer have the willpower;
No longer do I cry.

I've lost my self-respect for good
After years of self-abuse.
I've only got myself to blame;
I really have no excuse.

I've inflicted too much damage,
Empty is my soul.
I never thought I'd see the day
I'd be trapped inside this hole.

No energy left to fight it,
It beats me every time;
I can't control my weakness;
I'm just not worth a dime.

If I could have just one request
Before I finally crack,
The only thing I'd ask for
Is to have my innocence back.

But I know that will not happen;
It simply can't be done,
Though maybe in another life
If I am given one

Maybe I'll have one last chance
To try to right the wrongs,
And put my faith in Jesus
Where I think my heart belongs.

Only the Lord above will know
If I should be forgiven.
But will I be so fortunate
To meet with him in heaven?

I've nothing else to cling to,
He is my only hope;
And if I know he's guiding me
Then I know that I will cope.

But till I have the strength in me
To stop the demons calling,
The only way that I will go
Is down, for I keep on falling.

Fame

If you were ever famous,
There's something you should know:
People will follow your every move
No matter where you go.

With fame there's always money;
You can afford expensive things.
But sometimes fame can turn on you
And heartache is all it brings.

As long as you're level-headed
And don't get carried away,
Fame can be a wonderful thing;
It depends on how you play.

Fame can be used in a positive way,
Unless you're just a clown,
And instead of being sensible
You're always going to town.

If I was ever famous,
I'd always stay the same;
I wouldn't change my character
Just because of fame.

Farting

Why do I always get slagged for farting?
I can't help let go when I feel one starting.
A bodily function, like the beating heart;
But I get funny looks when I have a good fart.

Maybe, occasionally, they might just smell;
When I let one go, I'm told I'm not well.
When I have a dodgy tummy, be ready for a blitz;
There's nothing worse than a case of the two bob bits.

Some keep them silent, some let them belch,
But I can't resist a big watery squelch.
When I get picked on, I just say, 'Don't start!
I enjoy the pleasure of a really nice fart.'

People will say my behaviour's a farce,
But I just can't help my big squelchy arse.
I'll have to go now; I feel one starting.
Unless you want to hear big Davie farting!

Final thoughts of a Dying Man

I lie here bored and helpless,
Absolutely bed-bound,
It seems this will be my life
Until I'm buried in the ground.

I'd like to be more useful,
But it's not meant to be.
I can't wait for the day to come
When my spirit will be free.

There must be something better
Than rotting day by day.
I just want to leave this life;
For this I really pray.

It shouldn't be too long now;
I feel my body tire.
I just hope that when I go
It isn't to the fire.

My life has not been perfect,
Nor is it free of sin.
Although I have asked forgiveness
I'm not sure if it's been given.

I wish I'd lived a perfect life,
But I somehow lost my way.
Most of it was black and white
And very little grey.

So many wrong decisions;
I should have done much better.
Now I ask for mercy
In this poetic letter.

I hope my soul is cleansed
Before I leave this life;
Not really knowing
Cuts me like a knife.

In another hour or two,
This heart of mine will cease.
And, when that moment comes,
I hope that I'm at peace.

Flowers

I went to buy some flowers;
They're for the one I love.
A lovely bunch of roses
For my little turtle dove.

She likes to get the flowers –
She shows it in her face
(Although I do surprise her
In many other ways).

But flowers are the ideal gift;
They are a sign of romance,
And when my girl receives them
She gives me a loving glance.

Perfect for all occasions,
They're never out of date.
Giving someone flowers
Makes them feel just great.

For ever Last

Many years ago we lived in Possilpark,
We were happy youngsters – do you remember, Mark?
We didn't have a care way back then;
During summer we played out till way past ten.

We played football in the street;
It didn't matter who won, or who got beat.
We played for fun – do you remember, mate?
Although you and Mick could have been great.

You were both quite natural; do you remember, scan?
That's why you ended up with the nickname Johan.
We didn't have worries, we left it to others,
Thank God we both had really good mothers.

I didn't want those days to end;
I bet you didn't either, did you, my friend?
But in our hearts we knew those days wouldn't last;
The time just seems to go by so fast.

I think we're lucky we're not growing up there today,
We may have turned out a different way.
With all the crime from all the thugs,
Possil's now famous for problems with drugs.

But I'd rather remember those bygone days,
When Possil was a real safe place.
Playing out for hours on end;
Thank you, Mark, for being a friend.

I know those days are in the past,
But for me, my friend, they will for ever last.

Forgotten Shoes

A mother and her son
Went walking down the street.
The boy turned to his mother
And said, 'Mum, I've got sore feet.'

The mother then turned to the boy
And this to him did say:
'You never have this problem
When you go out to play.'

The boy said, 'Yes, but Mother,'
(While scratching his curly locks)
'I usually have my shoes on;
And I'm only wearing socks.'

His mother looked bewildered,
Then turned to him and said,
'Go home and put your shoes on!'
And the boy, he quickly fled.

After a while, the boy returned;
His shoes were on his feet,
And the boy and his mother
Continued walking down the street.

From a Boy to a Man

I've suddenly grown up,
No longer a boy;
More interested in a woman
Than I am in a toy.

It didn't seem so long ago
I was one of the lads;
But now that I am older
I'm almost one of the dads.

Where did my youth go?
It just suddenly passed.
I guess I was wrong
To think it would last.

We grow up so fast;
Where does the time go?
I used to be innocent,
Now I don't know.

Those carefree days
That I used to have;
At least I can look back
And have a wee laugh.

But now I'm an adult
And I'm not so carefree,
And that's just the way
It's always going to be.

I'd like to go back
If only I can;
But I've had my time
From a boy to a man.

Funny Thing, the Mind

A dark cloud hangs over me,
It will not go away.
I don't know where it came from;
It just appeared one day.

It makes the world look darker,
At least it does to me.
Maybe when the clouds lift
My mind will be set free.

I feel I'm trapped within myself,
My attitude has changed;
But please don't think because of this
That I'm the slightest bit deranged.

I'm sure the cloud will disappear;
I'll be glad to see it leave.
Then things will look much brighter –
I cling to that belief.

It's funny how the little things
Can really get you down.
I used to be so happy
And enjoyed acting the clown.

But maybe that's the problem:
My life's just been an act.
But the one thing in my favour:
I haven't actually cracked.

Everyone throughout their lives
Usually will find,
That little things can bother you;
It's a funny thing, the mind.

Getting Old

Every time I wake up,
Another day I face.
These days, life seems to me
To be a constant chase.

Always playing catch-up
Never up to date,
By the time I start to get somewhere
It starts getting late.

So many things to do,
It sometimes gets me down.
When I eventually get to the bus stop
I've missed my bus to town.

No time to go there now
I'll leave it till tomorrow.
I'll need to make sure I do it
As no one else can go.

There's far too much to do,
And I never have the time.
I never had this problem
When I was in my prime.

The way things are going
A home help will need to be hired;
And I thought that I'd have too much time
After I retired!

I'm finding it hard to keep on top
Of every little chore.
I guess I'll have to face it:
I'm not a young man any more.

Glasgow

Glasgow's old and ancient past
Has a history that will always last.
It's something that I'm proud to say
Makes Glasgow what it is today.

This grand old lady that is the city
Never asks or looks for pity.
Despite the scars and sorrows faced,
She's never turned her back in haste.

Her people look to her with pride
From both sides of the River Clyde.
North and south, east and west:
Glaswegians really are the best.

Hardened, yes, but kind at heart;
From Glasgow we can never part,
Even if there comes a day
When circumstances take us away.

Our hearts will stay in this dear green place
For moving away is just a phase;
For us Glaswegians since we were weans,
Glasgow's for ever in our veins.

Glesga Pattur

A wis born in Glesga
Menny yeers ago.
Springburn and then Posso
Ur the places a wid grow.

Playin roon the back
Of oor auld tenimint buldin,
Rakin froo the midgie bins
Wi awe the other chuldrin.

Playin fitbaw in the street,
Even lassies waanteed tae play.
'Weer no playin wi lassies –
Noo beetit, go away!'

Peepo fote they wur gallis
Wi awe the Glesga pattur.
Sumtimes yi gote the hardnuts
Lookin fur sumdae tae battur.

Tryin tae chat up a burd
Wi awe this Glesga lingo,
That mite hiff sumfin tae dae
Wi me stull bein singo.

Anyhow, aff gote tae go;
Aff sade anuf fur noo.
Time tae flush awe ma pattur
Doon the bluddy loo.

God's Amazing Stars

Looking out of my window,
I stare at the big black sky.
There are so many stars up there,
I've always wondered why.

I wonder if they have a meaning;
Why do they exist?
People study them as a job,
Or a hobby they can't resist.

Maybe the sky is watching us,
With no 'if's, 'but's or 'why's,
And what we're really looking at
Are a hundred million eyes.

The Bible says a star was used
As a guiding light,
That it led three men to Jesus
One dark and distant night.

Or are they all just planets
Like Saturn, Jupiter and Mars?
Whatever they are, I love to watch
God's amazing stars.

Goodbye

You're leaving me, then, or so I've heard.
Is it because you thought that I never cared?
Or is it because you've had enough?
Am I not the person you used to love?

I wish you would stay; things will improve.
Will you think it over before you move?
Or is your mind made up and there's no turning back?
Would staying for longer just make you crack?

You've been a good friend most of my life,
And I remember the day you became my wife.
I took you for granted, I know I was wrong;
I've been set in my ways for far too long.

Do you remember the days when we would dance?
I'm begging you now for one last chance.
But I'll understand if you decide to leave;
You'll have other goals you'll want to achieve.

I've held you back; I was at fault.
Now it's my life that's come to a halt.
But may I just say before you go:
As long as I live, I'll never feel so low.

I hope you don't mind if I have a wee cry.
I'll really miss you. Take care and goodbye.

Goodbye, My Dear Wife

You've decided to leave after twenty-three years
And you wonder why I am showing these tears?
I've done no wrong; you just want another.
But why did you have to move in with my brother?

Behind my back, so much went on,
Then, out of the blue, you've suddenly gone.
I could understand if I had been cruel;
Instead you've just made me look like a fool.

I love you so much, I don't understand.
Does it mean nothing to you that ring on your hand?
I could understand it if I'd given you a reason
But I did not deserve this act of treason.

But what can I do? I can't make you stay.
I can't stop these games you now want to play.
I hope that you're happy you shattered my life.
I'll be lonely without you. Goodbye, my dear wife.

Guilty

Your Honour! I stand before you
An innocent man.
Please don't give me
A driving ban.

I thought I was insured
When the officer stopped me.
It was out by a few days:
Just two or three.

As for the tyres –
Illegal, you say?
I was just on my way
To renew them that day.

As for the tax,
Well, let me explain:
I couldn't get to the Post Office
Because of the rain.

As for the other matter,
As I told my QC,
I really didn't know
It was a false MOT.

So you see, Your Honour,
The fault wasn't mine.
All I deserve
Is a very small fine.

But you turned out to be
A very hard man,
With a thousand-pound fine
And a one-year ban.

Hair

What's happening to my hair?
It's quickly falling out.
It's looking like a baboon's arse,
And that's without a doubt.

But it really doesn't matter,
I couldn't give a damn.
It doesn't matter much to me
If I'm called the 'baldy man'.

People who let it bother them
To me are only vain;
I'd rather have my health
Than be called a 'baldy bain'.

People seem to worry,
Thinking it's not fair,
But it's not the end of the world
If you lose a little hair.

You don't have to hide it;
I feel it must be said.
Just look at those two brothers:
Remember Right Said Fred?

If I win the lottery
I'll do a Highland jig.
But even though I'm going bald
I wouldn't buy a wig.

So don't judge people on their head,
Even if it's bare.
Look for their personality
Rather than their hair.

Handle with Care

Parcel just delivered,
I don't know from where.
All it says on the front
Is 'Handle With Care'.

Is it something made of glass
Of which care must be taken?
If it is, I only hope
It hasn't already been shaken.

Or maybe it's just plastic;
It's certainly light enough.
Whatever is in this parcel
Mustn't be handled rough.

I guess it's time to open it,
Just to see what's there:
An ornamental teddy bear!
I'll handle it with care.

Highway to Heaven

As I make my way through the corridors of life,
There are obstacles in my way.
It's up to me to face these obstacles
And deal with them day by day.

It isn't always easy,
There are times it seems so tough;
But I'm determined to keep on going
Because good times out do the rough.

The good times I refer to
Come with the help of my family.
We are all very close –
What more can I say?

It's important to stay on a steady track,
Though at times I've fallen off it.
But I get myself back on again
By showing some true grit.

I'm hoping to go to the place above
When I leave this wonderful land;
I'm sure I'll get there with the help
Of the footprints in the sand.

I'll try my best to get there
With all the help that's given,
And, hopefully, when I pass away
I'll take the highway to heaven.

Hillsborough

Do you remember Hillsborough
And the ninety-six who died?
It was very sad to see;
I was one who cried.

The pictures in the papers
Were very cruel, I guess;
But that's what you expect these days
From the British press.

Not that I'm against it;
It had to be that way.
Let's hope we've learned a lesson
From that tragic day.

I went to lay some flowers
With a friend of mine.
I felt sorry for the real supporters,
Crying all the time.

Reading all the papers,
Amazed at what I'd seen,
Comforting the families
Were Kenny and the team.

If you visit Liverpool,
Don't be satisfied
Till you've been to Anfield
And prayed for those who died.

Homeless

So many homeless people
On the streets of Glasgow.
Are they on the street by choice?
Do they have nowhere to go?

Why are so many homeless
In 1998?
Seeing people live like this
Is something that I hate.

Everyone needs a shelter –
A place to rest their head –
Even if it's just a room
With a fire and a bed.

It's sad that in this day and age
This seems to be a curse.
But that's the way it is, my friend,
And it seems to be getting worse.

I do not think that anyone
Should be without a home.
I hope someday they'll have a place to go
And the streets no more they'll roam.

Holly

Holly

I know a little girl
Who is quite a little dancer.
She's very like her daddy,
Except she's not a chancer.

Holly is her name;
A lovely little girl.
She really does love dancing
And loves doing a twirl.

'Everyone, this is Holly,'
Her daddy says out loud.
Of his precious little angel
He is so very proud.

I hope you like this poem;
For me it's been worthwhile.
I wrote it just for Holly
With the lovely little smile.

Home from Home

Coming home after all these years
I feel a little lost.
It's not so easy to settle down,
As I'm finding to my cost.

I've really missed my family
After all this time.
I thought I was feeling homesick
But I guess I was feeling fine.

We all live our different lives
And go our separate ways;
It's harder than it used to be
To keep in touch these days.

There's so much more I should be doing
Than staying in one place;
To move away from family
Is surely no disgrace.

The one thing you appreciate,
As you go away and wonder:
Being far from your family
Does make the heart grow fonder.

No matter how far apart we are,
I'm sure that everyone knows,
Nothing can stop this family
From being very close.

You can always take some comfort
From the places where you roam.
Just make the best of what you've got
And make your home from home.

Hospital

Quite a long time ago,
When I was just a boy,
I was in and out of hospital;
I didn't have much joy.

First it was my bladder:
I was told it was infected.
The time I spent in hospital
I felt very dejected.

The next thing I was in for
Was a perforated eardrum.
The only way to describe the pain
Is to say it left me numb.

Then I had food poisoning;
I was very seriously ill.
In fact, I was very lucky
It didn't actually kill.

Then problems with a kidney:
I was on a constant drip.
When I desperately needed water,
I was only allowed a sip.

I suffered all this illness
Before I was fifteen years old.
'You're doing all your suffering now,'
Was what I was always told.

Little did I know, of course,
This was not the case;
Even as a grown-up
I'm in and out the place.

I guess I'm just unlucky
With the illnesses I've had;
Though, these days, with the nurses
Hospital's not so bad.

I have to leave!

The day has come; now I have to go,
But first you really have to know
That I have loved you all my life,
Since the day you first became my wife.

I know you'll be left all alone;
I'm sorry to leave you on your own.
Tell me that you'll be all right
Before I go this very night.

I guess no more I'll see your face
Until we meet in another place.
No longer does my body breathe;
I'm sorry, but I have to leave.

I miss my Mum

I miss my mum very much;
I miss her warm and gentle touch.

I miss her talking on the phone;
I've never felt so alone.

I miss her funny little ways;
These are long and lonely days.

I miss the jokes she thought were funny;
Now she's gone it's never sunny.

I miss her more than you'll ever know;
Why did my mum have to go?

I miss her voice, her buckled hands.
I miss her buying the Kwik Save brands.

I miss her more than words can say.
I miss her each and every day.

A brilliant mother, a faithful wife;
I miss her precious little life.

I'm sorry if this is sounding glum;
It's only because I miss my mum.

I Never Thought!

I never knew just what you meant
Until you passed away.
I never thought I'd feel like this
But I miss you every day.

I never thought to tell you
How much you really meant.
I never thought to cherish
The times that we had spent.

I never thought to say to you
You had the greatest love.
I never thought to come to you
When I was feeling rough.

I never thought to mention
The happiness you brought.
Please forgive me, Mother;
I just never thought.

I Understand

I understand just how you feel;
I understand your pain is real.

I miss you lots and love you so.
When you look at me, does it show?

I understand the difficult years
When you brought us up; there were no fears.

All you got was moan, moan, moan
While you were struggling on your own.

I understand you're remarkably strong;
You always taught us right from wrong.

Although sometimes we've gone astray,
There's one more thing I want to say:

When I see the swelling in your hand,
Believe me, Mum, I understand.

Independence

Could Scotland survive on its own
If we got our independence?
Would breaking up the United Kingdom
Really make much sense?

We are a well-off nation;
I suppose it could be done.
It would be up to the politicians
To make sure that it's well run.

Or would it be a big mistake,
Should we leave things as they are?
Why should we now rock the boat
When we've done all right so far?

I think it would be better
To try to go it alone;
We could have our independence
And make it on our own.

Us Scots, we are a proud lot
The time is near, alas!
It's time we were treated as number one
And not as second class.

So when the time comes around,
We all can take our chance
And get ourselves to the ballot box
And vote for independence.

Inspiration

Where do I get my inspiration
To write the poems I do?
I get it from my mother
For whom I've written a few.

She told me they were really good,
And always gave me praise;
And now writing poems
Is how I spend my days.

I need to be inspired
Or I just couldn't write;
I even find I'm writing
In the middle of the night.

Other things inspire me;
Maybe a book I've read.
To me, it's very important;
It's how my mind is fed.

When my head is empty,
I really feel frustration.
It's then I have to look to life
To get my inspiration.

It's Just a Game

Don't be bitter because of a game.
I'm not like that; I wish you were the same.
We're both human beings who love our teams,
But you're far too serious – at least, that's how it seems.

I love the Celts; you love the Gers;
But if they lose now and again, who the hell cares?
No one's more passionate for their team than myself,
But I was very shocked at the attitude of yourself.

The banner of hatred you flashed in my face:
You thought it was funny; I thought it was a disgrace.
With my hand on my heart, this I can say:
Bigoted behaviour is not my way.

We're both human beings who live in the same land,
But because of my religion you won't shake my hand.
I respect your passion, there's nothing wrong with that,
But there's no need to act like a bigoted twat.

I know there are bigots who support Celtic as well;
But to me they are scum who should burn in hell.
To me, your a person who I certainly don't hate,
So don't be bitter when you could be a mate.

I understand your emotions will show
Because you want so much to get ten in a row.
I know you're a decent person; I am the same,
And remember, at the end of the day, it's just a game.

Legends of Rock

Remember Eddie Cochran, and his 'Summertime Blues'?
For him to die so young was really sad news.

Even Buddy Holly died a young man too;
Famous for his glasses, and singing 'Peggy Sue'.

Jerry Lee Lewis would never seem to tire
Of belting out the classic 'Great Balls of Fire'.

Twanging with the 'Guitar Man', guitar at the ready,
Playing instrumentals was Mr Duane Eddy.

Bill Haley and his Comets really loved to rock,
They sang many classics, like 'Rock Around the Clock'.

Gene Vincent and Fats Domino really got a thrill,
Singing 'Be-bop-a-lula', and 'Blueberry Hill'.

Chuck Berry could always put you in the mood,
Singing his classic 'Johnny B. Goode'.

And Elvis Presley, put his heart and his soul
Into becoming the king of rock and roll.

Letter to a Friend

Hello, dear friend, how are you?
There's something I must say:
The results from my doctor
Have been confirmed today.

I'm not looking for pity;
It isn't what I'm wanting.
I'm just a little worried;
My road ahead is daunting.

It's not too much to ask for
To lean on someone's shoulder,
To help me make some sense
Of why I'm feeling older.

When I was diagnosed with cancer
My life just fell apart.
I've tried being positive
But I haven't got the heart.

A sentence is placed upon me:
A month or two to live.
Just to be here for longer,
Anything I'd willingly give.

I don't feel ready for going,
But I know I'm going to die.
I know I'm not alone in this
So no longer do I ask why.

Life

Held within these prison walls,
Freedom is mine no more.
I committed the crime of murder;
Now I'm locked behind this door.

Let me have my freedom!
I cannot live this way.
No one seems to hear me;
I do not have a say.

Echoes all around me
From many other voices.
They also fall on deaf ears;
Can no one hear the noises?

Treated like an animal
By all these prison warders.
But they just say they're doing a job;
They're only following orders.

I'm here because I stabbed a guy;
I was stupid to use the knife.
I've twelve long years to regret it,
Now I'm in here doing life.

Life on the Street

So you think my life is wasted?
Well, I will prove you wrong.
I'll get my life on track again
And I'll do it before too long.

Spending time in the gutter
Has really made me think.
No longer do I want this life
Where I'm always on the brink.

These streets I walk have been my home
And I know I should feel shame,
But I really have to tell you
I feel I'm not to blame.

It was my circumstances,
Which I could not control.
Many things have happened;
That's why I'm in this hole.

I won't go into detail,
But I'm sure you'll work it out.
You only have to look at me
And there can be no doubt.

No one should have to live this way
But many people do;
But for the grace of God
It could even happen to you.

But I will sort my life out
Or death I might not cheat.
Anything would be better
Than my life on the street.

Light at the End of the Tunnel

The light at the end of the tunnel,
Will it ever appear?
I hope someday I'll see it,
I hope that day is near.

I need to get out of this darkness;
I've been here far too long.
I'm afraid of what might happen,
Something might go wrong.

I've been struggling all my life
Without a great deal of hope.
But somehow, when it matters,
I always seem to cope.

Looking for the light;
It must be coming soon.
Will it be sometime tonight
Or tomorrow afternoon?

Expecting it to happen
Is probably a big mistake;
But, if I haven't that to cling to,
No more could I take.

Meantime, I'll just carry on,
Morning, noon and night,
Until one day I'm out of this tunnel
And at last will see the light.

Little Bird

Fly south, little bird!
Fly away from here.
Time for you to migrate
For another year.

Spread your wings, little bird,
And fly high in the sky.
I wish you didn't have to go
But I know this is goodbye.

The climate keeps you on the move,
So you cannot stay for long.
It was nice to hear you in the morning
When you whistled out your song.

Will you ever come back again?
I can only sit and wonder.
But for now you must go, little bird;
I sense there might be thunder.

So please take good care, little bird;
I know you have no fear.
And I hope you and your offspring
Will visit again next year.

Little Rodent

OK, little rodent:
Tell me what you want.
I will give you anything,
If you'll leave this place you haunt.

There must be other places
Where you can roam about.
There's nothing for you here
But still you seem to doubt.

The thing is, when I have company
And they turn on the light,
If they were to suddenly see your face,
You'd give them such a fright.

So disappear, my little friend,
And stay away for good.
Now I hope you don't ignore me
Because that is very rude.

So I'll say this to you one last time
For I've really had my fill:
The next time that I see you here
I'll phone up Rentokil.

Loan Shark

I need to borrow money
To see me through the day.
Borrowing from a loan shark
Seems the only way.

They give you money quickly;
You do not have to wait,
But when it comes to paying them back
There's an added interest rate.

You have to pay them back on time
Or they warn you with a threat.
Things get very risky
If you can't pay back the debt.

These people do not mess about;
They are ruthless, through and through.
Using violence to get their money back,
That is what they do.

So if you can't pay your electric bill,
Just sit in the dark.
Or you might regret the day
You borrowed from a loan shark.

Losing You

I hope I didn't hurt you
When I shut you out my life.
I know I was really selfish,
Even though you were not my wife.

I know you think I used you,
And my actions were unfair,
But I just couldn't help it;
Deep down I really care.

My head is really mixed up;
I know you think the same.
Even though I hurt you,
I also feel the pain.

You think I'm talking nonsense,
But I'm speaking from the heart.
It's hard for me to say it,
But now I've made a start.

If I wasn't so confused inside
We might still be together.
But I know the actual fact is
I've lost your love for ever.

I hope you meet another
Who'll give you more than I.
I truly am so sorry
And I'll regret it till the day I die.

Lost Innocence

I remember when I was innocent.
It seems so long ago.
I've learned so much about life
I wish I didn't know.

I've changed as I've got older;
It's just a fact of life.
But somehow along the way
I cut my heart out with a knife.

I could have kept my innocence
Before I lost my way.
But I cannot turn the clock back
No matter what I say.

I cannot blame another;
The faults all lie with me.
I could have picked the proper route
But I pretended not to see.

It should have been so different;
So many plans I had
To do many, many good things –
Instead I did the bad.

When it's time to meet my maker
And my last breath has been taken,
It's then I'll have my innocence.
For I'll never be awaken.

Lost in Space

The Americans and Russians dominate space;
What are they doing in that dark place?
They are not just up there looking for Mars;
Are they planning a battle among the stars?

Floating about in outer space,
Looking down at the human race.
Shuttles and rockets sent to the moon;
I won't be surprised if we're all there soon.

Other planets will be explored,
With all respect totally ignored.
Whatever the Americans and Russians have found,
They should leave it there and get back to ground.

Do they really know what they could face:
That the day could come when they're lost in space?

Love (A Dreamer's Poem)

My love for you is endless;
It really has no ending.
I've really fallen in love with you
There's no point in pretending.

Please say that you want me
As more than just a friend,
And I will keep on loving you
Until the very end.

I remember when I caught your eye;
I knew you were the one
To bring me lots of happiness
And hopefully a son.

Maybe we'll have a daughter;
That would be just magic.
But if we couldn't have a child
It wouldn't be so tragic.

If that were to be the case,
There's always another option.
And maybe if you fancied it
We could always try adoption.

You know I really love you,
So will you be my wife?
And we could be together
And have a happy life.

Although I wrote this poem
With a lot of meaning,
Unfortunately for me,
I'm really only dreaming.

Lucky Little Cat

I am a little friendly cat; I come and go as I please.
I don't bother the mouse that always eats the cheese.
I'm just so friendly to everyone I see –
For me, it's the only way to be.

My master spoils me with a smile;
It makes my nine lives so worthwhile.
When he first saw me, he was totally smitten;
I was a very lucky little kitten.

I can stay out all day, it's really great;
It gives me a chance to find a mate.
Then I'll head home before I tire,
And get nice and snug in front of the fire.

A good night's sleep in my basket bed,
Then I prepare for another day ahead.
A wonderful life, and that's that;
I'm such a lucky little cat.

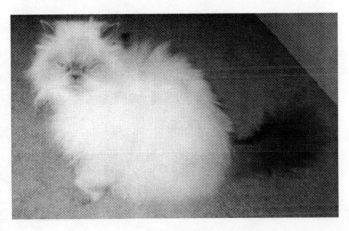

Maggie

Maggie was ill on New Year's Eve,
And from this world she was about to leave.
But that brave wee hamster was going to wait,
Until she made it into 1998.
And after the bells on New Year's Day,
Sean's wee friend peacefully passed away.

Marriage

Marriage is a blessing
Between people who are in love.
Both should always stand by their partners,
Especially when times are tough.

It's a really big commitment
You're meant to keep for life;
This is what it means
To be a husband and a wife.

Problems may occur,
Putting on some pressure.
But the marriage must come first;
It's something you should treasure.

When you take your vows,
To which you say 'I do',
Staying together for ever
Is what you're meant to do.

To have a happy marriage
You both must play a part,
And love each other always,
And mean it from the heart.

Max (My Faithful Friend)

I guess the time is coming, my faithful friend,
You haven't got long to go.
But just before you leave me
There's something you should know.

There will never be another like you;
You've been faithful to the end.
My heart is slowly breaking
To see you go, my friend.

You were always there to greet me,
When I came through the door;
Tail going crazy
As you raced around the floor.

Your companionship will be sadly missed;
No other can take your place.
I know that you are dying, my little friend,
I can see it in your face.

You will go to Doggy Heaven
But I really can't pretend,
Because every day without you
Will be hard, my faithful friend.

Goodbye, Max.

Missed Chance

I've seen your face so many times,
But only inside my head.
I've never seen you in person,
So I imagine you instead.

You'd be a lovely person;
Trustworthy, honest and kind.
If I could ever meet you,
That would really be a find.

You're someone I would cherish
And love my whole life through.
I'd be for ever happy
And hope you would be too.

You'd always care for others.
A heart that was so caring,
You wouldn't at all be selfish
You'd spend your life just sharing.

Well, that's the person I'd like to meet;
I know they must exist.
But since I haven't met her yet,
I guess my chance is missed.

Mother

The person most important in my life
Is my mother.
For love, respect and a tower of strength
There is no other.

A wonderful person, you hear me say;
A mother to me, to friends she's May.
Three daughters, seven sons; she must be proud.
I love her very much, I want to say it out loud.

It's not been easy, oh God, it's not,
But I am grateful for what I've got.
From youngest to the oldest brother
And a very, very special mother.

She sometimes gets very sad;
I wonder if she thinks of Dad.
Mother, if I can be so bold,
You also have a heart of gold.

Have I said thanks? Well here's another:
Thank you, and God bless you, Mother.

Motorway Madness

Driving on the motorway
After finishing work.
Someone driving far too close;
What a stupid berk.

Speeding down the outside lane;
Surely this is bad?
Why do people do these things?
I suppose it's 'cos they're mad.

They don't take any notice,
Even when it's wet.
There's going to be an accident,
That's a certain bet.

I've seen a lot of pile-ups;
I always think it's cruel.
If only they would take their time
And learn the two-second rule.

No matter how much sorrow,
No matter how much sadness,
We'll always get these stupid berks
Causing motorway madness.

Mr One Cup

Off he strolls to the kettle;
Will he fill it up?
What a disappointment!
Enough for just one cup.

Derek, will you listen?
There's more than you drinks tea.
There's Tam, Jackie and Denise,
And also there is me.

It doesn't really take long,
Just another minute or two.
Because what you should remember, Derek,
We always do it for you.

So, Derek, don't be selfish;
Try to fill it up
Or you'll always be remembered
For being Mr One Cup.

Mr Perfect

OK! So I was wrong.
Do you have to be so smug?
You get pleasure from my mishaps;
You're nothing but a slug.

You think that you are perfect
And that everything is wrong with me.
Well, I might not be perfect,
But I wouldn't want to be.

I like the way I am;
I wouldn't wish to change.
Acting any other way
Would make me feel so strange.

The way I act is natural;
I know no other way.
But you still try to bring me down
When you have your little say.

What you should remember
Is that things can turn around.
At least, in my experience,
That's what I have found.

But if that were to happen
I wouldn't stoop so low,
To laugh at your misfortune,
For life is not a show.

I hope one day you'll realise
The fool that you once were.
And maybe you'll find it in your heart
To finally start to care.

Must keep Warm

In wintertime it gets so cold,
It can't be easy for the old,
Trying to cope with freezing weather;
Many are at the end of their tether.

Just for the sake of having heat,
Some will go without food to eat.
They shouldn't have to live this way;
For heat, they shouldn't have to pay.

They need to have both warmth and food;
I'd make it law if only I could.
But the government just don't seem to care;
They feel the old should pay their share.

That's all right for the ones who have got,
But what about the ones who have not?
Many are freezing; it's just a disgrace.
This is something they shouldn't face.

To me, our old folk have the right
To have plenty of heat day and night.
During the cold or the threat of a storm
The old and the frail must keep warm.

Mum

Mum

You gave us life and loved us so.
We were precious to you; you helped us grow.

Your life was hard but you never complained,
Even when you were physically drained.

No one else could take your place;
Your little wave, the smile on your face.

We dreaded the day we'd have to part;
We've all been left with a broken heart.

You gave your all, your heart and soul.
We'll for ever have this empty hole.

The pain you suffered was far too much;
We'll always miss your gentle touch.

Thank you, Mum, for everything you've given,
You're with Granny now, up there in heaven.

From all your family, our love we send;
Our love for you will never end.

If we're lucky to go where angels fly,
We'll meet again – till then, goodbye.

My Head is spinning

My head is spinning,
I'm feeling dizzy.
In the pub
I have been busy.

My head is spinning.
Never again.
I should have stopped
When I got to ten.

My head is spinning.
I don't feel grand.
To be quite honest
I can hardly stand.

My head is spinning,
I'm feeling sick.
I guess the booze
I'll have to kick.

My head is spinning.
No more drink!
With a head like this,
It makes you think.

My lovely Bride?

I have just one thing on my mind.
Shall I tell you what it is?
It's just to get you on your own
And give to you a kiss.

This is what I long for,
And have done for a while.
The first time that I felt like this
Was when I saw you smile.

I know you might not fancy me,
So I've said nothing up till now.
But I couldn't stay silent for much longer;
My heart would not allow.

But if you do not feel the same,
Forgive me for what I've said;
I'll soon learn to accept it,
Though at first, of course, I'll dread.

These feelings I have inside me
I feel I have to share;
And if by chance you felt the same,
I'd be good to you, I swear.

But the chances are you'd hate the thought
Of being close to me,
For I hate the way I look myself,
So I know what you can see.

But it doesn't stop these feelings
I've always had inside,
Or the many times I think of you
As my lovely bride.

Never Mind

Living life as a millionaire
I really do enjoy;
Lying by my swimming pool,
Ferrari for a toy.

Constant sunshine all year round,
What a life I have found!
Private plane, servants too,
Sailing my yacht – so much to do.

Money takes me where I want to go;
To another country, or just a show.
All this money, all this wealth,
And I am in perfect health!

Wake up! It's just a dream.
That life for me will never be seen.
Back to the usual muck and grind;
It's only money – never mind!

News

Did you hear the news today?
It was very sad.
That little boy from Romania
Was left without a dad.

Just one of many thousands
Crying on TV;
In amongst the shooting,
For all the world to see.

A lot of heartache,
A lot of pain;
But their loved ones' deaths
Were not in vain.

They all stood tall –
And did you see
The people's faces
When they were free?

To all the reporters:
You did so well.
This gruesome story
Was hard to tell.

It's Christmas time;
You take no rest.
Let me wish you
All the best.

Number One

How blind I have been not to see,
In all the years you've been with me,
The beauty that you have within!
I could not see beyond your skin.

So much tenderness, so much love,
As if it comes from up above.
How could I have been so blind?
When, deep within, your beauty shined.

Someone else was on my mind
To make me be the selfish kind.
Only now am I able to see
This someone else was really me.

Never again will you be Number Two,
Because all I think of now is you.
You are so special for what you've done;
Now you're always Number One.

Old Photographs

Looking through old photographs,
Remembering days long gone,
Seems like only yesterday
But time has just moved on.

It's funny to remember
The days we used to have;
How it prompts the memory,
This old photograph.

It's nice to have reminders
Of many days gone by,
Of all the things that happened
To make us laugh and cry.

Old friends in the photographs:
I wonder where they are?
Have some of them passed away?
Do some just live afar?

Looking at these photographs
Reminds me of what I had:
Lots and lots of good times
And even a few bad.

I'll put them all away now;
I've enjoyed having some laughs,
Looking at these memorable
Old photographs.

Old Timer

How are you, old timer?
Is it true you were once a miner?

Did you work hard all your life
To support your children, and your wife?

You have a face that's seen it all;
Despite your age, you still walk tall.

You are a credit to the human race;
I know your boots I couldn't lace.

You've survived a war and much, much more;
I'm sure there's many times your heart was sore.

From you there's so much I could learn,
But first, your respect I'd have to earn.

This old folks' hospice where you are at,
I like to visit for a chat.

Take care, old timer. I'll see you again.
You're one of life's fantastic men.

Omagh (A Town Shattered)

When I heard about the Omagh bombing
I really was disgusted.
These are heartless bastards
Who can never ever be trusted.

Their only intention
Is to kill and maim.
They are nothing but scum
Who have no shame.

Those innocent lives
Are gone for ever,
Because these murderers
Want a blood-filled river.

The people have suffered;
The young and the old.
Dying loved ones
In their arms they hold.

How could anyone
Have done this deed?
Victims' families
Are left to bleed.

The people of Northern Ireland
Should suffer no more.
Their hearts have been shattered
To the very core.

We pray to God
All violence will cease
And the people of Ireland
Can live in peace.

Once Divided

Scotland was once divided
Many years ago.
We fought amongst each other,
Our countryman was our foe.

Battles between the clans,
The fighting went on at length.
It would usually end in victory
For the ones who had more strength.

Was the fighting really necessary
Between our very own?
I just can't understand it
But maybe I'm alone.

The Campbells and MacDonalds,
Just to name a few,
Did not like each other;
That's why the hatred grew.

But that was many years ago;
Times have changed since then.
Now we are a nation
And all the clans are friends.

To learn about our history
Is something I decided,
Just to find out for myself
Why we were once divided.

Only Five

They say I'm only five years old,
That is what I have been told.
I can't be older 'cos I'm only small
And to be older than five I would be tall.

Very soon I'll be starting school;
We have to go as a rule.
Lots of children will be there,
Lots of learning we all will share.

We have to listen so we can learn,
Little stars we have to earn.
At the swimming we have some fun.
We're taught to swim; it must be done.

I see kids jump and I see kids dive.
It won't be me; I'm only five.

Out of the Darkness

Come out of the darkness
And come into the light.
You will find the light much better
Than the darkness of the night.

To stay inside the darkness
Is not a good idea.
It's much better in the light
Where things are much more clear.

The darkness is depressing,
The light is where you're free.
Once you're out of the darkness,
Your path is clear to see.

Staying in the light
Is down to your state of mind.
But if you keep being positive
You'll leave the darkness behind.

Pain

Pain is something I live with
Every single day.
I've prayed for it to disappear
But it will not go away.

I don't know what I have to do
To free me from this pain.
Just when I start to get relief
It returns to me again.

I'm really at my wit's end;
I cannot take much more.
My moral is at rock bottom;
I can't get any lower.

I feed myself with painkillers
Till they're coming out my ears.
They do not take my pain away
And I've been taking them for years.

I've tried so hard to stop myself
From wishing I was dead,
But being in this constant pain
Just messes up my head.

Have I done something to deserve this?
I always seem to ask.
But I don't get any answers;
It's such a useless task.

But you don't have to worry,
My life I'll never take.
I'll keep my faith in the Lord above
And just hope to get a break.

Paradise

Tell me about the guy above,
The one who gives out lots of love.
Are you sure he does exist?
Then I hope that I am on his list.

I believe you're questioned at the gates,
Where they'll know your likes and hates,
All your bads and all your goods;
They'll even know of all your moods.

His place is known as paradise;
It's where someone goes when they die.
Unless, of course, we're unfortunate to go
To the other place that's down below.

To avoid this place we would do well;
No one wants to go to hell.
If it's true what they say and these places are real
I hope to the Big Man I do appeal.

When my time comes and I shut my eyes,
I hope I'm destined for paradise.

Parents

Only those who have the right
Can tell us what to do.
No one else can tell us,
Only the privileged few.

They can tell us any time they want;
When they do, we must obey.
And, since they're in complete control,
We must do what they say.

If we don't do what they tell us,
Things can get quite rough.
Especially if those who are in control
Start to get really tough.

Usually most of us have two;
If not, there's usually one.
If you're asking who we are to them,
We're a daughter or a son.

Please Don't Judge

The way I look I cannot help,
It's just the way I am.
Do not judge on what you see
Until you know the man.

An armless man can still embrace
If you get to know him face to face.
A legless man might not walk
But it doesn't mean he cannot talk.

A handicap does not mean danger
But you still decide to remain a stranger.
So please don't judge on what you see;
It's such a pathetic way to be.

I don't judge you; I would not dare.
But a friendly chat I'd like to share.
I'm a human being; inside I suffer,
So please don't judge me by my cover.

Pressure

I feel the pain, I take the strain;
It's all to do with pressure.
Even when I've finished work
It affects me in my leisure.

Every day I feel the same,
As if I'm feeling stress.
I try to put a brave face on
But I think my life's a mess.

Pretending to be cheerful,
Pretending to be glad,
When all I'm really feeling
Is usually very sad.

I wish I had a change of luck
And a little bit of pleasure,
If only for a day or two
So I can forget about this pressure.

Pretend

Did you once know me?
Was I once your friend?
And if I was not,
Then could you pretend?

I need you to help me;
I'm down on my luck.
Could you do me a favour
And lend me a buck?

It's just for a coffee
To help me heat up.
You're welcome to join me
If you fancy a cup.

You may wish to say,
'Just leave me alone.'
If that is the case
I'll just have a groan.

Are you sure you don't know me?
Think hard, my dear friend.
I guess you are right;
Why should you pretend?

Puppet

I am not a human
And I am not assumin'.

I have no heart
And I am not smart.

I can only stand
If I have a hand.

I cannot grow;
I am just for show.

I am not a he
And I am not a she.

I cannot speak
And I cannot keek.

I cannot love;
I am like a glove.

I am not a muppet
But I am a puppet.

Raging River

A stream of water flows along,
Soon it joins the river.
This is just a natural thing,
It's been like that for ever.

One day, the skies opened up;
For days the rain came down.
The river could not cope with this
And many were to drown.

The force of Mother Nature:
We can't control her rages.
The countless lives she's taken
And has done through the ages.

Dams are built to tame the river
But dams just can't compete;
The raging river bursts them open
And the dams are in defeat.

No matter how much man will try
To cope with nature's force,
It's best to get to safety
And let nature take its course.

Rhyme

What will I do
If ever there comes a time
When I try to write a poem
And I run out of rhyme?

I can't begin to imagine
The affect it would have on me,
For it gives me lots of pleasure
To rhyme my poetry.

Although it's just a pastime,
It's one I love a lot.
Anyone can do it
And you don't have to be taught.

You don't have to use rhyme
But many poets do.
It's whatever you feel right with,
It's entirely up to you.

So if you want to write a poem,
Write it from the heart.
I always find that doing that
Is the perfect way to start.

I'll finish off this poem now,
As I'm running out of time,
And I'll put my faith in God
That I never run out of rhyme.

Sad Dog

You look so sad, my little friend,
Tell me what is wrong.
Is it that you've been in here
Just a bit too long?

No one seems to want you;
Is this why you are sad?
It's not as if you bark a lot
And I'm told you're never bad.

You're not a little puppy
But you still look cute to me.
I want to take you home, my friend,
Where you can run round free.

I'll take you from this kennel,
Which I know has been your home,
And the first thing I will do for you
Is treat you to a bone.

Saddam's War

Somewhere in the Middle East
There's a dictator some would call a beast.
What he's done is an utter sham;
Who is this man they call Saddam?

Is he evil or is he mad?
He makes many people very sad.
Soldiers' families in despair,
But this man doesn't seem to care.

Another country, his men attack;
He is the dictator of all Iraq.
Why is he so filled with hate
He'd attack his neighbours in Kuwait?

Many want the war to cease,
But he must go, before there's peace.
What he's done is very cruel;
But, then again, this man's a fool.

There is one thing we know at least:
He'll never rule the Middle East.
Just one more thing that must be said:
Like Adolf Hitler, we want him dead.

Many deaths – and just what for?
One man's pleasure, to fight a war.

Say it Again

'Where are you, you dirty rat?'
Would say the little man.
I was listening to someone playing piano
And asked would he 'Play it again, Sam'.

Another man had scratched his head
When his luck he tried to press.
His friend then said to him, 'Stanley!
Well, that's another fine mess.'

The bad guy thought he was really smart
As the cop to him did say,
OK, you piece of scum;
Go on punk, make my day.

Nowadays for famous phrases
There seems to be a lack.
You either hear, 'Don't push me',
Or don't worry, 'I'll be back'.

That's just a few of the phrases
That I've heard through the years.
I'll continue to listen for others
But for now I'll just say, 'Cheers'.

Scotland

Scotland is the place to be.
It's such a brilliant place to see:
From the town of Berwick, to John O'Groats
And the little islands with all their boats.

Kilts and bagpipes are our tradition,
But there's so much more in addition:
Beautiful countryside, hills and lochs.
Foreigners would say we're lucky Jocks.

From north to south, east to west,
Here in Scotland you'll see the best.
The finest whiskey ever tasted;
A trip to Scotland would not be wasted.

There's just so much to see and do
So why not come? It's up to you,
But if you do come, don't forget
It might just be a little wet.

Scotland's Greatest Bard

Robert Burns was Scotland's greatest bard.
His upbringing wasn't easy; in fact it was very hard.
His talent was special – the whole world knows it;
This remarkable man was an outstanding poet.

To Rabbie Burns, writing poems was just a canter,
Have you read his classic, 'Tam O'Shanter'?
He was born on the 25th of January 1759,
And is responsible for the anthem 'Auld Lang Syne'.

There are far too many poems to mention;
By the time I named them all, I'd be drawing my pension.
'To a Mouse', 'To a Haggis', and 'Halloween',
They're all in his books, there to be seen.

One of his poems, I have to say,
Is a real favourite of mine: 'Scots wha hae'.
He married Jean Armour, but was none the wiser;
Rabbie Burns was a real womaniser.

When put to music, the beauty shows,
Just like 'My Love is like a red red Rose'.
When it came to his real love he was very wary;
Remember his poem about 'Highland Mary'?

His place of birth was Ayrshire's Alloway,
And on the 21st of July 1796, he died that day.
That he died so young left our country scarred,
But we'll never forget Rabbie Burns,
Scotland's greatest bard.

Scotland's Story

Historical is this country,
Rich in buildings old.
The story of our history
Has many times been told.

Abbeys, cathedrals and monuments
And many other things;
Touring round this country,
So much joy it brings.

So many brilliant people:
Baird, Livingstone and Watt.
Heroes in abundance,
Too many to name the lot.

People come from all around,
No matter what the weather.
They want to know the history
That lies beneath the heather.

We are a proud old nation;
Our hearts are full of pride,
Not just for our cities
But all our countryside.

So, if you know of Scotland's story,
I'm sure that you'll admit,
Even if you're not Scottish
You'd like to be a bit.

Seasons in the Sun

Remember the song 'Seasons in the Sun'?
It was a hit in 1974.
The song was sung by Terry Jacks,
Though he didn't write the score.

I was twelve years old when I heard this song,
And I feel I must confide,
It reminds me of a guy I knew
Who committed suicide.

The song itself is about someone dying,
A man who's saying goodbye,
Lying on his death bed.
It nearly makes me cry.

I really love to hear the song,
Despite the thoughts it brings.
And there's something about the voice
When Terry Jacks sings.

It is a golden oldie,
A real hit from the past.
It's just one of those records
That was really made to last.

Although it brings back memories,
There's no damage done.
So I'll always love listening
To 'Seasons in the Sun'.

Secret Life

I cannot tell you of my secret life;
It's no one's business but mine.
It's best to leave things as they are;
At the moment everything's fine.

To let you know would spoil things;
At least, for me it would.
I'd rather keep it to myself;
For the moment, at least, I should.

Some day I'll get it off my chest
And the burden for me will ease,
But let me tell you in my own good time,
Of that I beg you, please.

The more you ask, the worse I feel;
I'll tell you when I'm ready.
Well, OK, if you really must know:
I still sleep with my teddy.

Shadow

You're always by my side
Everywhere I go.
You're there with every step I take
You're with me as I grow.

I never hear you complain;
You're always very quiet.
Everything I do in life
I've also seen you try it.

Although you're always there
I can only see you sometimes;
Maybe in a certain light
And always when the sun shines.

You're not another person,
But everyone should know
You'll always be a part of me
Because you are my shadow.

Shopping

Off I go to the supermarket
To spend a bit of cash.
I'll have to take my time;
It's not a trolley dash.

I need some fruit and veg
And some cheese and meat.
I've got to fill this trolley
With lots of stuff to eat.

Also need some Corn Flakes,
And some Bran Flakes too;
I've got to have some fibre
To help me in the loo.

I better check my cash
To pay for all these goods,
That's OK, there's plenty;
I'll get some frozen foods.

Guess I'll be heading home now;
It's time that I was fed.
A couple more things I need to get:
Milk and a loaf of bread.

A big queue at the checkouts;
Someone must be ill.
There are six bloomin' checkouts
But only two girls on the till.

Silence

So silent is the dead of night;
Not a sound I hear.
Everything seems so peaceful,
But not for long, I fear.

It's fast approaching morning
When the birds begin to sing,
But all I hear is silence
Until my alarm starts to ring.

If this could last for ever,
This silence that I hear,
There wouldn't be any reason
For me to have an ear.

But silence only seems to last
When I am sound asleep,
And, then again, it only works
If the sleep I'm in is deep.

For the slightest noise can wake me up,
So I need my peace and quiet.
And if I'm wakened from that sleep
I'm grumpy! I won't deny it.

So I'll just enjoy this silence
As long as it may last.
For morning is soon upon me
And my silence is in the past.

Skint

I used to have a bob or two,
Never short of cash.
Nowadays I spend my time
Looking through the trash.

What happened to my money?
Where did it all go?
I didn't bother to save it.
And now I've nothing to show.

If I'd been a great deal wiser
I'd probably be worth a mint.
Instead I went and spent it all
And now I'm totally skint.

Sleepless

Feeling very tired
But just can't seem to sleep.
I don't think it would even help
If I started counting sheep.

It's not that there's something on my mind
That's keeping me awake;
I just can't seem to fall asleep
And there's no sleeping pills to take.

As I write this poem
I'm starting to drift away,
So if I cannot finish it now
I will another day.

Well, here we are, the very next day
And my promise I'm going to keep,
I'll finish off this poem now
Because last night I fell asleep.

Slow down

Slow down, please – you're going too fast –
Or else this journey could be your last.

Why do you feel you have this need
To get somewhere at the fastest speed?

It's a dangerous weapon, this car you drive.
Slow down now, and stay alive.

How would you feel, if you got into a skid
And ended up killing a kid?

It would be too late to sit and cry
If, because of you, someone was to die.

So kill your speed or it will be too late,
For the consequences would be far too great.

So slow down now and use your head,
Or someone's going to end up dead.

Please take note of what I say,
And hopefully no one will die today.

So Vain

I'm so good-looking
I just can't help myself.
With my looks there's no chance
I'll be left on the shelf.

I'm absolutely gorgeous,
Such a handsome hunk.
I only attract the beautiful girls
Not the other junk.

My life is just so perfect:
Good looks and lots of cash;
Wearing all the latest fashion,
Looking very flash.

Why am I so handsome?
I really have been blessed.
If I was on the stock market
In myself I would invest.

I've such a perfect body,
The envy of all my pals,
And when I hit the clubs
I'm eyed by all the gals.

I really can't help boasting;
It's how I made my name.
I'm afraid I just can't help it
If you think I'm really vain.

Soaps

Like a very strong magnet
We're drawn to these shows.
Why do we watch them?
Nobody knows.

First we have *Neighbours*,
The soap from Down Under,
That hit our screens
Like a crash of thunder.

They got rid of *Crossroads*,
And you wonder why?
I've seen better acting
From pigs in a sty.

One of the best
For wit and for charm,
Has to be that of *Emmerdale Farm*.

Why don't the Aussies call it a day?
With soaps like *Prisoner*,
And *Home and Away*.

Please take the high road
To Scotland and hide
From all of these soaps,
Including Channel Four's *Brookside*.

The first and the best
Which the others can't beat
Is most peoples favourite:
Coronation Street.

Spaceship

Look at all the gadgets!
It's like something from outer space.
And what's that thing at the controls
With the weirdest looking face?

It really is a spaceship
That's landed here this night.
But it's not what I expected;
I didn't get a fright.

The aliens are harmless;
They just seem a little lost.
They've landed on this planet
On this night of freezing frost.

I wonder where their home is,
And which planet they are from.
Maybe they have children,
Or miss their dad and mom.

They're on their way back home now;
I hope they get home safe.
I'll just wait here till they go
And give them all a wave.

Suddenly my eyes are open,
I've woken from a kip.
I guess I was only dreaming
About seeing that spaceship.

Staying Silent

You stand there in silence,
As you do every day.
Why do you never
Have anything to say?

Have you no voice
To say what you feel?
Would you speak to me
If I made you a deal?

Are you just silent
Because you are old?
Or is it thoughts of the weather,
Especially when cold?

You see passers by
Day in and day out;
If you want to be heard
You only have to shout.

But remaining silent
Is all that you do/
You live in George Square
And you're a big statue.

Talking to a Ghost

I can't see you, but I know you are there,
And I think your purpose is to try to scare.
Or are you just harmless? Maybe you are,
And I'm just being a little bizarre.

Are you a dream or are you for real?
Are you hanging on for a better deal?
Your spirit remains, though you are dead;
This is really weird, it must be said.

Is there a message you're trying to pass on?
Could that be possible once you have gone?
I'll keep it to myself, I wouldn't want to boast;
People will think I'm mad, talking to a ghost.

Tell Me

Tell me where you're going;
Tell me where you are.
Tell me all your troubles
Before you go too far.

Tell me in total confidence,
Tell me as a friend.
Tell me in your own time
But tell me before the end.

Tell me you're not dying,
Tell me it's not true.
Tell me it's someone else you know,
But tell me it's not you.

Tenement Kid

A Glasgow tenement was my home
When I was just a kid.
I played 'shop' with broken glass
Like many others did.

As the years passed along,
It was football and pushing tyres.
And once a year it was a thrill
To see the burning bonfires.

At Easter time a hard-boiled egg
Was rolled down some hill.
Although you never see it now
Then it was a thrill.

At Christmas when the snow came
Down the stairs I ran.
I guess I wasn't the only one
Who wanted to build a snowman.

The well-off kids got choppers,
Or chippers for the wee ones,
But I was happy with my cowboy outfit:
A belt and two toy guns.

When it rained, we played inside the close
Making lots of noise.
What do you expect from a tenement kid?
Remember, we were only boys.

The Beatles

Remember the Beatles?
Who could forget?
Thank goodness McCartney
And Lennon met.

The songs they wrote
Were absolutely brilliant.
They both must have been
Very resilient.

With George Harrison
And Ringo Starr,
The Fab Four
Went very far.

The most successful group
There has ever been.
And there was tough competition;
Know what I mean?

They'll always be remembered
For the music they brought.
Thanks to the Beatles;
You'll never be forgot.

The Black Sheep

I've always been the black sheep,
Or so I have been told.
My kin they have disowned me;
I'm not quite in their mould.

I've been shut out for many years;
I didn't have a say.
But I knew in time, eventually,
I would have my day.

When I came back from years away,
My father stared with shock.
Why have you returned this day?
Do you come here just to mock?

I said that I had missed him;
He looked at me with doubt.
It's then that I reminded him
It was he who'd shut me out.

'I never wanted to go away,
But you didn't want to keep
This son who always loved you,
So you branded me the black sheep.'

The Bully

He always acts the hard man
And thinks he has a right,
Together with his buddies,
To pick on people to fight.

He always picks the weakest,
Someone who won't fight back.
It seems to give him pleasure
To humiliate and attack.

He's nothing but a coward;
He needs his pals before he's brave.
He has respect for no one
And doesn't know how to behave.

He acts like he's a gangster,
But he's just completely dim.
I wonder how he'd like it
If someone picked on him.

A bully is a scumbag;
I guess they're all the same.
I hope someday they realise
And hang their heads in shame.

The Clown

Behind your mask there lies a sadness
But you wish to hide it away.
There's nothing wrong with showing your feelings
You'll find that out someday.

The painted face forever smiles,
But what lies underneath?
Remove the paint and show the world
A face that's full of grief.

It's nothing to be ashamed of
To have suffered a broken heart.
Reality is the real world
Not that of Billy Smart.

We all try to hide our feelings,
Especially those of sadness,
But sometimes letting them build up
Only leads to madness.

I'm asking you to remove the paint
And let me see your frown;
And I will help you smile again
Because, to me, you're more than a clown.

The Clyde

We are so lucky to have the Clyde,
This river that is Glasgow's pride.
Ships were built in bygone days;
Our ships once ruled the waterways.

Times were tough and men worked hard,
Working many hours in the yard.
Clydebank was an industrial town
For building ships was its renown.

But now those days are in the past;
Building ships was not to last.
The days of shipbuilding have since passed by
But the spirit of the Clyde will never die.

This famous river that is the Clyde
Will always remain Glasgow's pride.

The Countryside

Somewhere deep in the countryside
Is a life so far away.
I hope that I can have that life;
Maybe I will someday.

Away from all this hectic living
Is where I want to be.
For me, being in the countryside
Is where you can be free.

The countryside, it has so much;
You can also live off the land.
There's little chance of shops and stores
Being close at hand.

I hope one day I'll get the chance
To leave this life behind,
And move out to the countryside
Where happiness I'll find.

The Cruise

Sailing on the ocean waves
On a ship that's so majestic.
It's not quite the *QE2*
But it's still quite fantastic.

Cruising all around the world,
This really is a dream;
Being treated like royalty
By the captain and his team.

It really is a pleasure
Floating on the sea.
Nothing all around for miles,
Feeling completely free.

Relaxing on the top deck,
Feeling the summer's breeze;
What a joy it is to be
On the seven seas!

I'll remember this cruise for ever;
Great memories I have had.
If I could only do it again
I really would be glad.

So if you can afford it,
What have you got to lose?
Rather than lie on a sunny beach,
Book yourself a cruise!

The Day I nearly died

While rock climbing in the Lake District,
I tripped and nearly fell,
Eighty feet above a stream;
I was staring down at hell.

Luckily, I managed to get a grip
And stop myself from falling.
My friends had wondered what was wrong
And soon I heard them calling.

'It's OK!' was my reply
As my heart was pounding quickly,
But that was just a little lie;
I was really feeling sickly.

When I got down to the bottom,
I just felt such relief.
That really was the last time
I'd give myself that grief.

I haven't climbed another rock face
And probably never will.
I'll stick to something safer,
Like climbing up a hill.

Every time I think of it,
The death that I defied,
I just can't get it off my mind,
The day I nearly died.

The Devil in Me

I can't control the devil in me,
He's stronger than I thought.
He makes me do these stupid things
And one day I'll get caught.

When I am at my weakest,
That's when he gets a grip.
He takes control of my senses;
Bad thoughts I just can't skip.

I always try to fight him off
And, for a while, I might succeed.
But soon he's back inside my head,
Like an ever-growing seed.

I know there is an answer
To deal with all this stuff;
He's stronger than the devil:
He is the Lord above.

But will he want to know me
After all the sins I've done?
Though deep inside I really know
God forgives everyone.

I'll seek to find my master,
And hope he'll understand
That what I'm really looking for
Is for him to take my hand.

I really need his guidance
To help to make me strong.
But I know it's in my own hands
Because I do know right from wrong.

I'll really try to change my life,
And rid this evil into the past.
But I know until the day I die
The fight will always last.

The Drunk

Walkin' doon a Glesga street
Ah tripped and had a fall.
Somedae said Argyll Street
But ah think it was Sauchiehall.

Ah canny quite remember;
Ah wis a wee bit worse for drink.
Am trying ma best tae remember
But ah need some time tae think.

Noo, let's see: ah came oot the pub
And staggered doon the road.
Ah wis tryin tae pretend ah wisnae drunk
But ah guess it must huv showed.

Ah only went for a couple a pints
But must huv been in for ages.
Noo that ah come tae think of it,
Wit did ah dae wi ma wages?

The wife will dae her nut
If ah go hame like this.
She'll no listen tae reason;
She'll jist gimmy a Glesga kiss.

Ah'll huv tae tell her ah got mugged
And the muggers nicked ma loot.
But she'll probably dae wit she usually dis
And jist fling me oot.

Wit am ah gonny tell her?
Noo, let me huv a think.
Ah guess while ah work it oot
Ah'll go and have a drink.

The Emerald Isle (a Scot's View)

Travel to Belfast on the ferry,
Then head for Bangor or Ballykelly.
Dublin city is beautiful and fair;
The memories of Ireland you'll want to share.

See Dundalk and Tipperary,
And visit Killarney and the ring of Kerry.
In this beautiful land of the shamrock,
You can go on a pilgrimage, to the shrine at Knock.

When in Ireland, you'll have a ball,
Going to Cork and Donegal.
The people are friendly, this I can say;
I found that out in beautiful Galway.

Of places to visit, there are many,
Including Limerick and Kilkenny.
The Irish welcome you everywhere,
In Ballymena, Omagh and Kildare.

On the way back home you'll have a big smile,
Having enjoyed yourself on the Emerald Isle.

The Face that's in the Frame

There is a picture in a frame;
I thought it might be you,
But if it turns out not to be
I can only wonder who.

I feel I know the person
Whose face is in the frame.
Unless it's my imagination
And the face is not the same.

The picture in the frame is old,
Hence the black and white.
But I think I've seen the face before,
I'm sure that I am right.

But maybe I'm just dreaming
Of a face that's in my head.
Or maybe it's a face I used to know
And now the person is dead.

I hope you'll take me seriously,
For this is not a game.
I honestly feel I've always known
The face that's in the frame.

The Fire inside my Heart

You are the one I most admire;
For you I have a burning fire.
It burns so strong inside my heart,
And even more when we are apart.

My love for you will never die;
It just gets stronger as days go by.
Is your love for me just as strong?
If so, together we do belong.

Or does your heart hold no place?
Would you rather forget this ageing face?
If that is so, I wish you well,
But I can't pretend it won't be hell.

To lose your love would be much too hard,
When all this time you have starred.
But I feel your love is just as strong
And these thoughts I have are simply wrong.

The life we share is so worthwhile,
I can tell by how you always smile
The fire in your heart is always burning
And so our love just keeps on turning.

And so until this earth I part
The fire will burn inside my heart.

The Gate

Silence fell upon me
As I walked through the gate.
Was this to be my destiny?
Was this to be my fate?

I don't know what to make of it.
It's not what I expected.
I need a little time
To get my thoughts collected.

It seems a little spooky
Being here by myself.
I'm not sure if the experience
Will be much good for my health.

Maybe I should turn around
And walk back out the gate.
But I don't think that would do much good;
I've left it much too late.

My curiosity brought me through;
I didn't heed the warning.
Coming through the gate
Was a big mistake this morning.

The sign said 'DO NOT ENTER';
The consequences are great.
I hope I don't live to regret
Walking through the gate.

The Great War?

I've heard about the Great War
From many years ago,
But many lost their lives
And now they're buried low.

They fought with so much courage
Until they could fight no more;
Such a loss of life
We only can abhor.

Barely seventeen years old;
So young to face a war.
Many would not return alive;
What was it all for?

I'm told peace is the answer,
The reason for all the dying.
But peace is still not with us
After all the years of trying.

It seems to me the men in power
Feel the need to fight,
But it isn't them who face the bombs
And are blown out of sight.

The men who fought for their countries,
And the women too,
Will not stop other wars
Where the soldiers could be you.

We have to find an answer
Or everyone will perish.
And that is not a thought
I really want to cherish.

For if we have another war,
A war we all would hate,
Would people be saying in years to come:
'Boy, that war was great'?

The Great Western Road

Driving out of Glasgow
On the A82,
Within half an hour
You'll be admiring the view.

Head for Loch Lomond,
And relax for the day,
Or just carry on
Up the West Highland Way.

If you think you've gone
A little too far,
Stop and have a rest
At Arrochar.

But if you keep on driving
And stay on the go,
You'll soon see the mountains
Of lovely Glencoe.

Pass through Fort William
Till you get to Loch Ness,
And very soon you'll be
In Inverness.

The Job

First, I get my pad
And see what's planned today:
An early-morning lesson!
I must be on my way.

I look at all my hours,
And guess what I can see?
Is it ten or twenty?
Oh no, it's thirty-three.

My pupils think I talk too much,
They think that I'm a pest,
But they always say I'm brilliant
When they pass their test.

I like to tell a joke or two
And think I'm a reasonable chap.
Then I say, 'Wasn't that funny?'
They say, 'No, it was crap.'

Well, time for me to go now,
And that, my friend, is no lie.
So, until we meet the next time,
Let me say goodbye.

The King (of Rock 'n' Roll)

He is the King of Rock 'n' Roll,
Elvis is his name.
He died in 1977;
Bingeing and drugs were to blame.

He sold millions of records
And still does today.
He's probably sold more records
Since he passed away.

He's the most impersonated music artist
Ever to be done.
But when it comes to Elvis
You know there's only one.

From 'Heartbreak Hotel'
To 'Moody Blue';
From 'Jailhouse Rock'
To 'The Wonder of You',

Did he ever imagine
What his success would bring?
Did he ever imagine
Being called the King?

But the King he was
Of rock 'n' roll.
Elvis Aaron Presley,
God rest your soul.

The Life I Seek

A life that is worth living
Is a life I'd like to have,
Not a life that makes you cry;
But a life that makes you laugh.

A life not full of heartache,
But a life that's full of joy.
A life that gives me all the things
I pictured as a boy.

A life that has no evil,
A life that sees no crime;
Just a life of freedom,
Not a life doing time.

A life that's full of good things
That everybody had;
A life where your mother
Is loved by your dad.

A life I could be proud of;
Is this too much to ask?
I guess you have to work at it
But I wasn't up to the task.

My life should be much better,
But I have been too weak.
But that's the life I really want;
That's the life I seek.

The Man on the Moon

The man on the moon has disappeared.
I wonder where he's gone?
The moon is also disappearing
As the time approaches dawn.

Maybe I'll see him tomorrow night;
He's probably taking a rest.
Even he must need a break;
It happens to the best.

I wonder if he's lonely,
As he walks around the moon.
Maybe one day others
Will join him up there soon.

I wonder how he feels
Up among the stars,
Far away from his family.
Will he have emotional scars?

He'll always be my hero –
That will never change –
And I know a lot of people
Will probably think I'm strange.

If I wrote to him a letter
And sent it by balloon,
I wonder if it would ever reach
The man who's on the moon?

The Meaning of Life

Do you know the meaning of life,
The reason we exist?
Are we just a part of
An ever-growing list?

Some get into debt,
Just to live in style;
Some will meet a partner
And walk them down the aisle.

Some are good Samaritans,
Helping those in need.
Some of us are selfish
And live a life of greed.

Some might be disabled
Or blind, or cannot hear;
Some are maybe bullied
And live a life of fear.

What is the meaning of life?
Why are we alive?
We do everything in our power
Just so we survive.

We all have our troubles,
We all cope with strife;
It's all just a part of
The meaning of life.

Music from the Past

I love the golden oldies, the music from the past:
Rock 'n' roll and jive, and the music was made to last.
Known as the Fabulous Fifties, the guys wore drainpipes
    and Brylcream,
Living in that fabulous era must have been a dream.

Then the Swinging Sixties, from the Stones to the Fab
    Four,
And then the time of Woodstock, where it was hippies
    galore.
Britain gave us Cliff, America gave us Elvis,
He was the King of Rock 'n' Roll, and known as Elvis the
    pelvis.

Then we had the seventies – platform shoes and flares –
If you wore that gear today, you'd get some funny stares.
I really loved the music, the highlight being glam rock;
But Wombles and Smurfs having hits, well, that was just a
    shock.

Not everything was popular, there were a fair amount of
    shockers,
And the seventies were certainly famous for giving us punk
    rockers.

And then we had the eighties, a change of music and style;
Some of it was OK, some of it was vile.
Although there were some good bands – the Minds, U2
    and the Cars –
There were also a few rotten ones, singing out of their arse.

Now we're in the nineties, anything becomes a hit.
OK! There are some good songs, but most of them are
    shit.
Well, I've nothing more to say, so these words are my last:
You just can't beat the oldies, the music from the past.

The Piano

I am an old piano
With black and white keys.
Will you do me a favour
And tickle my ivories, please?

I'm jazz, I'm classical; I'm rock or pop,
And once you start to play me you won't want to stop.
You can play me to words, or music alone;
Just play and enjoy my melodic tone.

If you can't play me, you can always learn,
Isn't it something for which you yearn?
If you learn to play me, soon you will grow
To love this old musical piano.

The Poem

If I write a poem
Does it have to rhyme?
People say, 'Of course it does!'
So I have to take my time.

I wouldn't say I'm gifted,
'Cos usually I'm just messing.
The fact that I enjoy it
Comes as just a blessing.

People seem to think it's hard;
I'm sure it's just a rumour.
All it takes to write a poem
Is a sense of humour.

You're wondering if I'm English?
No, my friend, I'm not!
I'm from a place called Glasgow
And proud to be a Scot.

The rhymes, they keep revolving
Like a wheel that turns.
But one thing I can say for sure
I ain't no Rabbie Burns.

The Radio

The radio is a great companion
Wherever you want to go.
You can listen to lots of music
Or maybe just a talk show.

You feel you know the presenters
Who do those radio shows,
But that's the strength of radio;
That's the way it goes.

No matter where you go in the world,
No matter where you've been,
Just listen to the radio
And the guys who can't be seen.

You can tune into AM
Where there is also long wave,
Or maybe just get FM
And listen to some rave.

And if you cannot sleep at night,
If you're feeling tireless,
Just listen to the radio;
It's what they used to call a wireless.

The Rich Man and the Tramp

There was this very rich man,
With more money than he had sense.
He wouldn't part with any of it;
He held on to every pence.

A tramp passed him in the street.
'Good day sir! How are you?
Could you lend me fifty pence
To buy myself a brew?'

'Go away you low-life beggar –
I hate the likes of you!
Begging on the street like this
Is all you ever do.'

'I'm sorry if I offended you
By asking you like that,
But do you really have to speak to me
Like I'm nothing but a rat?'

'You're worse than a rat, you low-life scum!
You should be lined up and shot,
Or, better still, put down at birth
But I guess no one had thought.'

As he stared into the beggar's eyes,
He saw the resemblance to his mother.
It's then that he had realised
He was talking to his brother.

The tramp was given away at birth;
His mother couldn't cope with two.

No one would adopt the kid;
Hard times he'd had a few.

The other one had everything,
Was spoilt and inherited riches.
His brother was unfortunate;
He ended up in ditches.

Would the rich man's attitude change?
Would he now embrace his brother?
But the only words that he would say
Were, 'Go and ask another.'

Greed was in his veins now,
Selfish to the core,
And instead of sharing his money
The rich man wanted more.

Rushing off across the road,
The tramp had made his way.
A speeding car had knocked him down
The tramp had died that day.

'Does anybody know this man?'
Someone said aloud.
But the rich man's voice was silent
As he stood among the crowd.

Despite his massive riches
He's now just old and sad;
If only he had embraced, that day,
The brother that he had!

He tries to search for comfort,
Turning out his bedside lamp.
Will they ever meet again,
The rich man and the tramp?

The Road of Life

This road is never-ending,
The one I walk each day.
I don't know where it leads to
But it's such a long, long way.

Even when I'm driving,
I still can't reach the end.
This road is really something
I just can't comprehend.

It's strictly one-way traffic,
So there's no turning back;
And for signs of where you're going
There seems to be a lack.

The road is long and winding,
With slip roads here and there.
But do you take the slip roads?
Only if you dare.

The road that I am speaking of
Isn't always nice.
You can only travel it one time;
You can never do it twice.

The few signs that do appear
Are there to help you out.
You can't ask for someone's help,
Not even if you shout.

The road is leading somewhere
Though not a place like Fife,
But somewhere more important,
For this is the road of life.

The Soldier

He hears the shouts of admiration
For a soldier who fought for his nation.
His friends are missing, blown to bits;
This happened during the Blitz.

He wonders why there are cheers and smiles
When the dead are counted in massive piles.
The mood is sombre inside his head,
As he thinks only of the dead.

Loved ones waiting, tears from crying,
Limbless bodies on stretchers lying.
Many blinded, cannot see;
Is this the way it was meant to be?

He has a lost and empty stare;
It's just the start of his long nightmare.
Eventually he'll be able to close his eyes;
It's then he hears the battle cries.

Rebuilding his life, where does he start?
How does he mend his aching heart?
All that's left amounts to zero,
And you expect this man to feel a hero?

The Storm

The winds blew fast,
The winds blew strong;
Trees were falling
What had gone wrong?

People in houses
Trying to keep warm,
While some on the outside
Were killed by the storm.

Seeing people struggle,
Hearing people shout;
And things were made worse
Because of a blackout.

Chimneys came down,
Causing a crush,
All because
The wind was in a rush.

You go to the council;
They give you a form,
To claim for the damage
Caused by the storm.

The Sword

It would glisten in the sunshine
As it was raised above one's head;
This dazzling piece of metal
That many people dread.

It's been used in many battles
Throughout many years.
It caused the death of thousands
And brought many fears.

The sword was used before the gun;
It was the ultimate weapon.
And there were many times
The sword was used to threaten.

The many who had used the sword,
Did they feel there was a need?
They must accept what happened to others,
That they would also bleed.

This weapon of destruction
Killed thousands, so I read.
It's not the sword that killed them
But man who did the deed.

The Telly

When you watch the telly,
Do you get confused?
Watching *Potter's Blackeyes*,
I'm totally bemused.

I nick off to the kitchen
For an appetizer,
Then get back to the telly
And watch *The Equalizer*.

When I watch the BBC
Relaxing in my seat,
I think I'm watching something new
But it's only a repeat.

They show a film for the seventh time
By Metro-Goldwyn-Mayer,
There's not a lot that we can do;
We're just the licence payers.

But never mind, the dinner's on,
It's warming on the cooker.
I'll just change the channel…
Oh no! It's bloody snooker.

There's lots of shows on satellite,
Both serious and funny.
The only problem is, my friend,
They're asking lots of money.

Now I've had my dinner,
I'm waiting for my jelly.
I know that I'll enjoy it
A lot more than the telly.

The Wild Sea

At times you are so gentle.
You wouldn't harm a fly,
But when you lose your temper,
That's when people die.

The anger as you batter ships,
And put them on alert,
Has many people worried;
That's an absolute cert.

You've taken many lives before,
Impossible to count.
And every day that passes by
The toll continues to mount.

No one can judge your temperament;
It's part of nature's way.
And, yes, I know the weather
Can have a lot to say.

I do not think you're evil
For all the lives you've taken.
It's really down to nature
That they have been forsaken.

Yet, still you are a marvel
And I know you always will be.
You'll always have my respect
Because I love the wild sea.

The Wreckage

Driving along a country road,
I came upon a crash.
Somebody was lying dead,
Their life gone in a flash.

Another was badly injured,
Lots of blood around.
Everything was quiet;
I couldn't hear a sound.

The man was trapped inside his car,
The sight was very shocking.
I tried to reassure him
And tried to keep him talking.

I said I had to leave him
To go to find a phone.
But the man cried out,
'Please, don't leave me alone!'

I really had no option;
Help was needed fast.
I had to call 999
Or this man wouldn't last.

When I got back to the wreckage,
He didn't move his head.
I tried to check for a pulse
But now the man was dead.

I've tried to carry on with my life
But I just can't turn the page.
All I do is think about
The bodies in the wreckage.

The Writer and his Book

I am the writer of this book;
Will you take the time to have a look?
I wrote it for you all to see.
It's the first one ever written by me.

It's a book of poems that's within these pages;
It can be read by people of different ages.
Many subjects have been covered,
Including some where people have suffered.

I've tried to add plenty of fun;
You'll find some humour in more than one.
Writing poems you express a lot,
All the different feelings you have got.

So I hope you've enjoyed having a look
At all these poems, from the writer and his book.

Thinking Back

I'm thinking back to my younger days;
There's memories good and bad.
But I preferred my life way back then,
When I was just a lad.

Growing up with all my friends
Gave me so much pleasure.
They were the best days of my life
And ones I want to treasure.

They really passed so quickly;
They were here and now they've gone.
Thinking of my childhood
Never makes me yawn.

Now that I am older
And whenever I have time,
I think about the old days
And all those friends of mine.

Despite the times of calling names
And taking lots of flack,
I still enjoy the quiet moments
When I am thinking back.

This Beautiful Land

I look at this tranquil land,
Its beauty and its splendour.
It's a place that is so natural
And really seems so tender,

A place that is untouched by man
And I hope it always will be.
When you're in the open air
You smell the freshness of the sea.

There are hills and lakes aplenty
And so much there to do.
Like walking, sailing and climbing
Or whatever satisfies you.

This place is just so beautiful;
It could be paradise.
Though I don't know if that comparison
Is really very wise.

But then again, if truth be said,
It really is God's land.
So if I call it paradise
I'm sure he'll understand.

At times I love to come here,
Just to get away from it all,
Because with this wonderful valley
In love I did fall.

And, as the saying goes,
I would give my right hand
So I could be for ever
In this beautiful land.

This Life

Into the world we come
With no cares or worries.
We start off with baby food
And end up with curries.

We're guided by our parents,
Who teach us right from wrong.
They have about sixteen years with us;
I'd say that's fairly long.

Then into the big wide world we go
To stand on our own two feet.
We try to find a job
Just to make ends meet.

If everything has gone to plan,
You're really on a roll,
And I guess if everything hasn't
You're probably on the dole.

Then we're meant to meet a partner,
A husband or a wife,
So that we can make babies
To continue on this life.

Tiger

This striped cat that hunts the land,
He is in search of food.
He'll hunt until he gets his prey
Like only a tiger could.

To build his strength and stamina,
A tiger needs to feast.
He is the ultimate predator,
This beautiful looking beast.

I love this brilliant creature;
Just to see it roam,
Not trapped inside a cage,
But in the jungle that's his home.

I hope they don't become extinct;
I've heard it said they might.
They should always be protected;
These tigers have a right.

I hope they survive for ever,
So everyone can see
This very beautiful tiger
That was born to be free.

Time

Time waits for no one;
It just keeps ticking on.
And time will continue to do so
Long after we've gone.

Many things will come to a stop,
But time just keeps on going.
That's why everything in this world
Continues to keep on growing.

Time's been here for ever,
Since the world began.
It's not controlled by machinery
And certainly not by man.

It's just the world revolving,
Turning night and day.
If anyone controls it,
It's God who has the say.

Time is very precious,
So we're always told;
Anyone who says it's not
Must be very bold.

There's many rivers to cross
And many mountains to climb.
It's something I will challenge
If I'm just allowed the time.

To a Loved One

To a lady called Maureen, I just want to say
I was shocked when you told me the news that day:
The death of your husband, the death of your son.
This is dedicated to a loved one.

I felt so sorry, because I knew you were sad
And then came another blow: the death of your dad.
Your friends are magnificent; we all need someone.
This is dedicated to a loved one.

Don't hold it in; I know that you'll try.
Sometimes we all have to break down and cry.
But when the rain's gone, up comes the sun.
This is dedicated to a loved one.

I'll say a prayer, and I'll say it with love,
Knowing they've all gone to heaven above.
I'll say one for you, consider it done.
This is dedicated to a loved one.

To find a Woman

The way to find a woman
Is to hit her with the charm.
It's the only thing to hit her with
As this will do no harm.

Once you have her within your sight,
You mustn't let her go.
Tell her she looks gorgeous;
That's what she want's to know.

Arrange to take her on a date,
Somewhere not too far.
Take her in a taxi
Or, better still, your car.

If the date has been a success
You're definitely on your way.
There's a really good chance
You'll see her another day.

If you become an item
And plan to set a date,
Make sure you're really certain
Before it becomes too late.

But if you're really sure
You want her in your life,
Don't be scared to go for it;
Ask her to be your wife.

I know I'm not an expert –
Like you, I'm only human.
But there's nothing wrong in giving my view
On the way to find a woman.

To Love my Life

One day I'll sit down and to myself I will ask:
'Why was my life such a hard task?'
It could have been easier if only I'd tried,
But I let myself down. Where was my pride?

I watched folk around me try hard to succeed
While I sat around; I didn't feel the need.
But how wrong I was! I must have been blind;
And so it's my fault that life was unkind.

At least if I'd tried this I could say:
'I gave life my best, but it just got away.'
But I was too lazy. I depended on luck;
And depending on luck just got me stuck.

Now I am sorry I have no success;
My whole life has been just one big mess.
You only get from life what you put in
And all of my chances I put in the bin.

If it's not too late, I'll have one more go
So I can look back at my life and have something to show;
And if I succeed I know I'll feel great
I'll look back at my life and no longer feel hate.

The whole world will seem a much better place
And I will constantly have a smile on my face.
I won't have the pressures and I won't have the strife,
And at last I'll be able to love my life.

To You

Your worth is more than I can say,
Your love gets stronger every day.
There are no limits to what you'll do;
You cheer me up when I'm feeling blue.

When help is needed, you're always there.
You're very special, the way you care.
It's time that you were number one
For all the things that you have done.

I know that words can't say it all,
So I've placed you on a pedestal.
For me, you're up there on your own;
You're very special, just you alone.

Transport

It started with a horse and cart,
Way back at the very start.

Times moved on, then came the tram;
They were never stuck in a traffic jam.

Buses, cars and passenger trains
And those big massive aeroplanes –

Many forms of transportation
Taking us from nation to nation.

Transport is really great, you see;
It gets us all from A to B.

Treat Him Well

If you're lucky enough to have a great dad,
And you can't remember him being really bad,
Treat him well.

If he's given you all his time and love,
And you can't remember him being rough,
Treat him well.

When he starts to grow old, and someday he will,
If he's unlucky enough to have fallen ill,
Treat him well.

If he's done his best all his life,
Or has a broken heart after losing his wife,
Treat him well.

You only get one father, as you do a mother;
Give him all your love and attention, like no other
And treat him well.

UFO

I looked up into the sky
And saw a flashing light.
I'm sure it was a UFO;
I really got a fright.

As this thing got closer,
I felt I had no choice;
I tried to turn my eyes away
But was deafened by the noise.

I know it was a UFO
That hovered right above,
But if I try to tell someone
They'll say my story's duff.

I believe that there are UFOs;
I saw one with my eyes.
But no one will believe me;
They'll think I'm telling lies.

Uninvited Guest

Please do not hurt me;
I mean you no harm.
If you just got to know me,
You would see I have charm.

I mind my own business
Here in your house,
Except, now and again,
I'll have a wee browse.

I openly admit
To not paying rent,
But I cannot tell you
From where I was sent.

I don't smoke cigarettes
Or drink your cider;
I'm just a wee, harmless,
Innocent spider.

Walk another Mile

Of all the miles I have walked
Along this rocky road,
There were many times I carried
A burden for my load.

At times this burden weighed me down
As I continued on my way;
Not just every now and then,
But nearly every day.

This burden that I carry
Will not hold me back;
Complete determination
Is one thing I don't lack.

At times I think of Jesus
And the cross he had to bear.
It makes me forget my burden
As if it isn't there.

So as I continue on my journey,
I just raise my head and smile.
Although I have my burden,
I walk another mile.

Wallace and Bruce

In 1297 we started the story;
In 1314 the scene was glory.
Edward Longshanks, a man without sense,
Tried to take our independence

William Wallace, a man of pride,
Cut down the English in his stride.
King Edward's army he would have slayed,
But to Scotland's shame, he was betrayed.

As Wallace dangled from the hangman's noose,
He thought of Scotland and the Bruce.
'Take up the fight and draw your sword;
You'll defeat the English, thank the Lord.'

Robert the Bruce took up the fight,
And fought the English with all his might.
With Edward's army he'd take his turn,
And slaughter them at Bannockburn.

All us Scots should say out loud:
'Of Wallace and Bruce we are so proud.'
Because of them, we're not England's slave;
That's why we're known as Scotland the Brave.

War and Death

I wonder what would happen
If there was ever a third world war.
Would everyone be killed this time,
And what would it all be for?

Weapons are far deadlier
Than they have ever been before.
The last war killed many millions;
This time it could be more.

No one would be a winner;
Everyone would lose.
It doesn't matter what people think,
We won't be asked our views.

All that we could expect to face
Is tragedy and fear.
Because, whether we would like it or not,
We live in a time of nuclear.

I hope it never happens
But I wouldn't hold my breath;
The thought of another world war
Where all we faced was death.

Our destiny lies with our leaders;
It's they who we obey.
But I pray to God none of us
Will ever see that day.

Wedding Day

The ring you wear this very day
Makes you full of joy.
You really do look happy,
Like a child with a new toy.

The dress is absolutely beautiful;
What more can I say?
You'll always have the pictures
Of this brilliant day.

You said 'I do' together
Earlier on today.
Tomorrow, it's your honeymoon
Where you both will make your way.

Who would have thought some years ago,
When you started with the kisses,
That you both would end up in the church
To become Mr and Mrs?

The reception was fantastic,
Family and friends all there,
And when we saw the wedding cake
Everyone wanted a share.

Today was such a lovely day
And there was quite a crowd,
And I know the man you married
Will make you very proud.

When one is

When one is sad tears will fall;
When one is mad you hear them bawl.
When one is happy they wear a smile;
When one is slow they take a while.
When one is fast it's because of speed;
When one is selfish it's usually greed.
When one is poor their hearts are sore;
When one is rich they just want more.
When one is kind they always give;
When one is free one will live.
When one is tired they have a rest;
When one is brilliant they're the best.
When one is king he'll be told he's great,
But while one is queen he'll have to wait.

Who will protect me?

Who will protect me from this hell?
It's with me every day.
Who will protect me in this life
When I cannot find a way?

Who will protect me when things are bad
And I have nowhere to turn?
Who will protect me when I'm cold and wet
And the fire will not burn?

Who will protect me from this evil
That lurks within my way?
Who will protect me with words of comfort
That only my mum could say?

Who will protect me from all the pain
That lies within my heart?
Who will protect me from all the danger
When trouble is about to start?

Who will protect me when I'm old?
Does anyone really care?
It's God who will protect me from all these things,
For He is always there.

Why?

It was a cold December night;
We should have been happy with Christmas coming up,
But we were in mourning for our little boy, James,
Who had been killed by a drunken driver.
His life hadn't even started
He was only seven years old. Why?

In a world full of heartbreak,
Suffering and pain,
We know that our lives
Will never be the same.
James was a happy and joyful little kid
But his life ended
Through what one driver did.

He said he was sorry
As he walked off unhurt,
While our little boy
Lay dead in the dirt.

For so many families who suffer this pain
And the thought that their lives
Will never be the same.
And still they ask: why?

These drivers are criminals,
The worst of their kind;
They know what they are doing
And they don't even mind.

But the law's got to change
And stop being weak,
And sentence these murderers to life.

But still this goes on, and still people die,
And still we keep asking: why?

Your Heart was with Somebody Else

We've been together for so many years
And I thought we were doing just fine,
But each time I told you I loved you
Your heart was with somebody else.

Why have you stayed for so many years
When it's clear you felt nothing for me?
I gave you all: my heart, my soul.
But your heart was with somebody else.

CHORUS

You decided to go to the one you loved,
And you left my world shattered and torn.
I understand now it would never have worked
For your heart was with somebody else,
Your heart was with somebody else.

MIDDLE EIGHT

So I'm the fool who stayed around;
There was you and me, what did I not see?
You told me I would get you down,
But when you looked happy, oh, it was him not me!

CHORUS

You decided to go to the one you loved,
And you left my world shattered and torn.
I understand now it would never have worked
For your heart was with somebody else,
Your heart was with somebody else.

Years had gone by since the day that you left
When you turned up, right out of the blue,
And you said you were wrong, you wanted me back,
But my heart is with somebody else.

CHORUS

I did love you once but I'll never forget
How you left my heart shattered and torn.
But I'm sorry to tell you I want you to go;
My heart is with somebody else.
Yes I'm sorry to tell you I want you to go,
For my heart is with somebody else.
Oh my heart is with somebody else.
Oh my heart is with somebody else.

Lisa

A sadder place this world will be
Now you've gone away.
You were always full of life,
Despite what came your way.

Life would test you to the limit:
Many times it kicked you down;
But up you got time after time –
Lisa's back in town!

You have to be admired
For the spirit you have shown,
And I know that there were many times
When you felt you were alone.

But on your own you never were;
Your family was always there.
They were with you every step of the way –
I've seen the way they care.

The laughter that would fill a room
I remember very much.
I wonder if you realised
The many lives you touched.

I love you and I'll miss you.
My heart is feeling sore
To know that on this earth
I will see your face no more.

But my heartache is nothing
To what your children feel,
For my heartache may end one day,
But theirs will never heal.

May God embrace you in his arms.
I'll see you there one day,
So keep the laughter I know so much
The Lisa Martin way.

Lisa

Amy Rose

Your lovely smile,
Your gorgeous eyes,
Your cheeky grin
Are no surprise.

Your curly hair,
Your gorgeous face;
You're a special girl
In many ways.

Your little stories
You always tell;
In personality you do excel.

You're one in a million,
Everybody knows.
Who else can it be?
It's Amy Rose.

Amy Rose

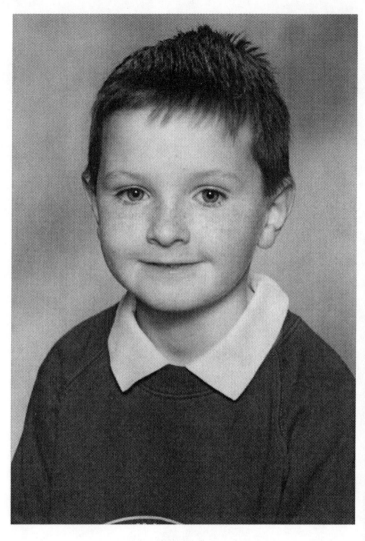

Kris

Kris

Carol and Eddie's little boy
Was my mothers pride and joy.
She loved her grandson very much,
He'll really miss her special touch.

But this wee guy won't have any fears,
Because he's got his Granny and Granddad Speirs.
This wee guy is so full of fun;
I love him as though he was my own son.

But when you look at him, you can see he's glad
That he has a loving mum and dad.
This wee guy is really bright –
If you say something wrong, he puts you right.

A piece of sausage and he is quite happy –
It's easy to please this wee chappie!
I used to call him a little muppet,
But he'd just turn round and tell me to shut it.

And if I try to tickle his leg,
He has the cheek to call me a big egg!
There's many people who love this wee guy,
He gets on with everyone and isn't shy.

I'll finish off this poem by saying this:
I love this wee guy, who's name is Kris.

Barry's Blanket

Barry's Blanket

I want to tell you about Barry
And the blanket that he has:
He's rarely seen without it
This cheeky chappie, Baz.

A constant wee companion
To my best friend's little boy,
Barry's little blanket
Is his pride and joy.

Although he has got Thomas,
His little choo choo train,
Without his little blanket
He wouldn't be the same.

So when he goes to bed at night
To sleep until the morn,
This faithful little blanket
Will keep wee Barry warm.

If I were a Millionaire

If I were a millionaire
I wonder what I'd do.
I could stop buying second-hand
And start buying new.

I could live my life in luxury,
Get people in to clean.
I could really take advantage
Of the millionaire scene.

I could have friends in high places,
Thanks to the money I had,
And there would always be a reason
To have parties in my pad.

My money could keep me happy,
Just knowing that it's there.
I wouldn't worry what people thought;
I just wouldn't care.

Would I really be like that?
Is that the way I'd live?
Would I keep the money for myself
Or would I want to give?

It wouldn't make me happy
To be a millionaire,
If I ended up as someone
Who just didn't care.